You Have Not Many Fathers

Recovering the Generational Blessing

Dr. Mark Hanby
with Craig Lindsay Ervin

©Copyright 1986 – Dr. Mark Hanby

All rights reserved. This book is protected under the copyright laws of the United States of America. This book may not be copied or reprinted for commercial gain or profit. The use of short quotations or occasional page copying for personal use or group study is permitted and encouraged. Permission will be granted upon request. Unless otherwise identified, Scripture quotations are from the King James Version of the Bible.

Take note that the name satan and related names are not capitalized. We choose not to acknowledge him, even to the point of violating grammatical rules.

Father's Heart Publishing
PO Box 369
Lewisville TX 75067

"Speaking to the Purposes of God for this Generation and for the Generations to Come"

ISBN: 978-0-692-65239-8

For Worldwide Distribution
Printed in the U.S.A.

Thirteenth Printing: 2016

This book and all other Mark Hanby Ministry and Father's Heart Publishing books are available at
www.yourquantumlife.com

Dedication

To Stanley R. Hanby, my own dear natural father and spiritual mentor who taught me to see God through the windows of nature and simple living. Upon giving me my first leather-bound Bible, he said, "Most anyone with normal intelligence can read what other men say and repeat it ... but if you make yourself a student of this one Book, they will all want to say what you say." However, through the years I have mostly wanted to say the things my father said.

Contents

Foreword vii
Prologue xv
Introduction xxi
Chapter 1   The Father's Dilemma 1
Chapter 2   The Father's Order 15
Chapter 3   The Father's Inheritance 33
Chapter 4   The Father's Heart 51
Chapter 5   The Father's Covenant 67
Chapter 6   The Father's Voice 89
Chapter 7   The Father's Maturation 121
Chapter 8   The Father's Garments 143
Chapter 9   The Father's Anointing 157
Chapter 10 The Father's Relationship 177
Chapter 11 The Father's Honor 195

Foreword

Our God is methodical. He is not chaotic. If we want to be prosperous both spiritually and naturally, then we must endeavor to know and function within His divine order. I am reminded of that truth whenever I read about the creation of our world as recorded in the Book of Genesis.

It is there that God, through His eternal wisdom, whispers in the ear of His servant the unveiled blueprint of the creation of the universe. When you read it, you are reading of the origins of history and the procession of events that marked the dawning of the world as we know it. It is here that God begins the order from which His methodical structure for all truth emanates and flourishes. For instance, He calls from the muddy montage of an uninhabited planet the herb, plants, and greenery. He brings forth these plants whose seed will reproduce and grow in the calm summer breezes of thousands of years.

And God said, Let the earth bring forth grass, the herb yielding seed, and the fruit tree yielding fruit after his kind, whose seed is in itself, upon the earth: and it was so **(Genesis 1:11).**

He will create only once the blade of grass with which He expects to garnish His fields. His plan is so futuristic that it puts within each plant a seed of potential. The seed holds the key to reproduction and thereby eliminates the possibility of extinction.

Each blade had a destiny created in its origin. Its future is perpetuated in the integrity of its seed. As long as there is a seed to germinate, the blade, through its progeny, will be represented. Its purpose cannot be aborted. It is this principle that governs all of God's creation.

In the same manner this concept maintains order in the universe—each entity producing seed. Whether plant, fowl, or fish, these life forms have survived through their ability to produce seed. I believe that these truths can be applied to some spiritual issues that we face in the spiritual kingdom. The natural order just reflects for us through metaphoric simplicity the greater issues of spiritual truths.

Howbeit that was not first which is spiritual, but that which is natural; and afterward that which is spiritual **(1 Corinthians 15:46).**

The way for our ministry to survive is predicated on similar concepts. It depends upon, is even built upon, the principle of father to son. If we are to have any lasting effect, we must understand the significance of this relationship as it affects the Kingdom of God. This area is one that the enemy would attack severely. He knows that the principle on which all of creation hangs, the principle God used to build nations, do mighty works, and even provide redemption, hangs on the relationship between a father and His son! What lasting effect might God do through us if we were to perpetuate ourselves through the strong covenant of a father to son? I would submit to you the firm concern that haunts the mind of many vessels across this nation. It is not enough to build great buildings. Neither will we be effective building great denominations. The nation behind the denomination is nothing if it is not built on the relationship of those within it. All lasting works will only survive as we cultivate the power of a father to his son.

God has assigned one of His finest vessels to lead us into the inner sanctums of an issue that has been neglected for far too long. Dr. Hanby brings to life the spiritual potentials that have been hidden from view. Our growth has been stunted by the lack of illumination in this provoking area. I believe gifts will be stirred and limitations challenged as we catch a glimpse of the spiritual offspring of true ministry. There is no way any leader can grasp these powerful truths and not impact his generation. A powerful release of ministry comes from understanding the reproductive relationship of ministry.

Who is my father?

This is the question that has troubled the hearts of many whom God would raise up in this hour. What constitutes a real father-and-son bond is a bewildering issue to understand. Many men have staggered across this country silently bleeding, wrestling to know and discover the strong covenant that should exist between spiritual fathers and their sons. It is these fathers whose loving-kindness and firm hands were meant to usher their sons of destiny toward their prophetic potential. Some sons even aligned themselves with men who lacked the heart to father and so have suffered abandonment and betrayal. How can we be a functional Church without healing?

Although it is true that many men have contributed to our education and spiritual enrichment, few of them have been empowered to impart to us the rich inheritance that God has promised. Like Benjamin, who received his prophetic name from his father, we have waited patiently. At last, God has sent a word that gives clarity to a complex issue that lies at the foundation of our identity. It is the name that declares the identity. Could it be that many have been functioning without a true sense of identity?

Benjamin was inappropriately named by his dying mother, Rachel. She named him Benoni, "son of my sorrow," but his father called him Benjamin, "son of my right hand," or "son of my strength." Out of his father's prophetic utterance came the lineage of King Saul, the first king who reigned over Israel. It is a tragedy for sons to misalign themselves to someone who cannot speak to their destiny.

Many of us have been misnamed in the dying arms of a Rachel-like system that named us on the basis of its own calamity. It is to those bleeding sons whose cracked identity and broken dreams have halted their growth, that I extend an invitation.

Come journey down the long dusty road to truth that brings us into the recognition of our fathers. It is here in their arms that we receive the name that unfolds destiny. The enemy has worked relentlessly to create a feeling of misplacement among those of us whose ministry and gifts have been tainted with a feeling of illegitimacy.

As one blade of grass gives seed to the perpetuation of its successor, we must recognize and value fatherhood. There is a deposit they can give that enables us to avoid the dysfunctions that have damaged ministries across the globe. It is important that these gifted men do not pass off the scene with their seed locked in the loins of untapped ministry.

There is seed to be sown from which there will be a powerful impartation. To the fathers I say, "Pour what you have into the next generation. Pass the baton into the hands of faithful men." Your ministry will continue to perpetuate itself through the lives of men who have felt the warm hand of your counsel and the rich seed of your ministry.

I also would caution every young man whose feet have begun to walk in the steps that God has designated. They must be careful, in their haste to become fathers, that they do not lose track of the inner need to have fathers. If it were possible, satan would leave each of us nameless and violated. Perhaps he has tried to leave you detached and disconnected. Sons must realize that the hands of the father release the blessing to them. Furthermore, we sons must acknowledge that our fathers have been empowered to convey the blessings we need. Like Israel, who sat up in the bed and strengthened himself (see Gen. 48:2), God has sent a strengthening word to enable the wayward son to receive the stabilizing blessing of his father. With it he will begin to unlock the purpose from which kingdoms are built.

For too long the Church has tried to reproduce through cold, sterile documents a relationship declared on paper that was not exemplified in reality. Real sonship cannot be transmitted through the joining together of men bound only by the cold bonds of a business decision or document. Consequently, many men are ships adrift. They are in need of a father's hand to bless them. They have longed for the investment that enables the dividends of wisdom to accrue throughout the ages. Sadly, they sense inside a void and a dearth of the true reproductive bond between fathers and sons.

No doubt life will afford each of us countless opportunities to be inspired. It will allow us opportunities to be enthralled by the eloquence of voices and the grandeur of speeches. Yet at the end of all these listless and lofty dissertations, there will arise a hollow ache from a longing heart. It is the hurt of a broken heart in a generation of divinely appointed men who realize that they have many teachers, but not many fathers.

It is my prayer that you receive insight and imparted truth as you eavesdrop on this conversation between the Holy Spirit and His servant. Dr. Hanby writes from the annals of wisdom that God has richly deposited in his heart. A man who has become a father for many men, he is, himself, a model of excellence and a mentor for those of us who are wearied from the blaring of many voices and many preachers. No disrespect is intended, but we have had many whose lips sputter truthful facts from cold fountains, and whose rusty faucets have been contaminated with the cares of this world. There are multiple places where we can go and receive from many teachers disconnected gibberish, cold statistics, and lofty quotations, but alas, when all is said and done, Dr. Hanby with the apostle Paul has well stated that we have not many fathers!

T.D. Jakes

Prologue

The purpose of these "before words" is to warn the reader that the truth contained in the following pages might be considered highly inflammatory and could cause an incendiary response in both "hot heads" and "burning hearts." Whenever the concepts of order, proper church government, authority in relationship, and honorable recognition are spoken of in the Church today, clanging alarm bells and screaming sirens drown out the urgency of the real emergency.

Many have been wounded by those who used the sword of God's Word to amputate and maim. Now they hesitate whenever the power of true revelation approaches. Malchus, the servant of the high priest, had his ear cut off by the hacking thrust of Simon Peter when they came to arrest Jesus in the garden. Like Malchus, some bleed from past apostolic wounds, unable to hear the truth. If that describes you, please do not allow past misconceptions to cloud present revelation. Do not let carrying the throbbing pain of former afflictions be a substitute for following the heartbeat of the Spirit. I pray that the words of this book would be a source of healing toward headship, in the same way the fingers of Christ restored the ragged ear of Malchus.

Although I have taught the order of fathers and sons for years, I always had a hesitation at being called a father in ministry myself because of these words of Jesus: "And call no man your father upon the earth: for one is your Father, which is in heaven" (Mt 23:9). This Scripture echoed within my heart every time someone asked me to be his spiritual father. Wanting always to obey the Word, I steadfastly refused my fatherhood.

This Scripture was opened to me when I understood it in the light of other biblical passages. Malachi prophesies that God "shall turn the heart of the fathers to the children, and the heart of the children to their fathers..." (Mai. 4:6). John the Baptist was sent "to turn the hearts of the fathers to the children" (Lk. 1:17). Paul refers to himself as a father to the Corinthians (see 1 Cor. 4:15), and indirectly pronounces his fatherhood every time he calls Timothy or Titus his son in the gospel (see 2 Tim. 1:2; 2:1; Tit. 1:4). The apostle John refers to three classes of individuals: little children, young men, and fathers (see 1 Jn. 2:12-14). If Jesus said, "Call no man on earth your father," and Paul and John both called people on earth "father" in the same Bible, then perhaps we have misunderstood the original meaning of the words of Christ.

The full text in Matthew reads: "But be not ye called Rabbi: for one is your Master, even Christ; and all ye are brethren. And call no man your father upon the earth: for one is your Father, which is in heaven. Neither be ye called masters: for one is your Master, even Christ" (Mt. 23:8-10).

This Scripture is not against referring to someone as your spiritual father any more than it is a commandment against calling your natural parent "father." It was a word to the Pharisees and religious people of Jesus' day who placed the words of rabbinical scholars and theological statements on the same level as Scripture. The Pharisees referred to the famous rabbis of the past as "the fathers." Hence, you have the references to "the fathers" in Stephen's sermon in Acts (7:44, 51-52) and the reference to fathers in Hebrews (1:1). Therefore, in Matthew 23:9 Jesus is referring to "Father" as God's ultimate authority in our lives and ministry. We must disavow anything (including doctrines of men) that exalts itself against the fatherhood of God. This is why the prohibition against calling a man your father is equal to that of calling someone your teacher or master. A spiritual father will never replace the authority of Scripture. Fatherhood on earth is simply a confirmation of "our Father which art in heaven."

Now, I do not foresee us following in the path of Roman Catholicism and calling every ordained priest a father as a title of office. However, I do think that in our protest against Rome, we have perhaps ignored a vital truth.

In addition, our discussion of fathers and sons is not one that excludes women in ministry. The concept of fathers and sons does not deal with gender, but with those spiritual inheritors of promise, both male and female. I truly believe that "there is neither male nor female in Christ" (see Gal. 3:28). The qualification for a woman in ministry is the same as for a man: There must be a connection to the house of a father. The Bible teaches that in the absence of a male heir, the daughters received the inheritance of their father (see Num. 27:7-9). The only stipulation for a woman receiving her inheritance is that she marry within the tribe of her father (see Num. 36:8). On this side of the cross, it is still necessary for a lady in ministry to be in proper alignment with her husband for spiritual covering (see 1 Cor. 11:4-5). Of course, this principle also is true concerning men who are called to be "husbands of one wife" (1 Tim. 3:12). The use of the terms *fathers* and *sons* in this book is not meant in any way to denigrate or deny the powerful roles that mothers and daughters fulfill in the Kingdom. The principles of ministry are true regardless of gender. It is both "your sons and your daughters" who shall prophesy (Joel 2:28).

Finally, upon presenting some of this material to my publisher and friends to peruse, I have been strongly advised of similarities between the truth contained in this book and what they refer to as "the shepherding movement." I have been told that these ideas create fear in many people because they were once caught in the controlling factor of messages from ministries that were so full of "father-type authority" that people were practically in bondage. For instance, they were told not to make any major purchase such as buying a car or laying carpet in a home without notification to and instruction from others over them in the Lord. This control extended to tragic and destructive interference in family relations where, at times, men even claimed they had conjugal rights to other men's wives.

That is not a father-and-son relationship at all. This flood of abusive leadership that swept aside the set boundaries of God has no basis in Scripture. This devastating abuse of authority to control and sinfully manipulate is sick and rightfully condemned.

Not only is the subject of father authority fearful to many, but the terms of *son* and *sonship* are quite alarming to others as well. There was at one time a doctrine referred to as the "manifest sons." This old message, which occasionally surfaced through the ages, found a new root system in the 1940's and 50's in America. This theory evidently stated that the manifest sons of God were an elite group of men who, through their perfection in becoming like Christ, were the actual incarnation of God in the world. Again, this is not what this book is stating at all. These people did not understand that we have the Spirit in measure and that becoming like Christ in the fruit of character is not becoming deity.

Much truth has been lost because it was shrouded in error. There may be a glorious flower blooming in a garden, but if the sun is in a certain place and a tree casts its shade, the blossom may be so shadowed that the beauty of its petals are unseen. Tragically, the truth concerning fathers and sons was hidden and lost in past years when God's efforts to bring this truth to light were shrouded by man's own misconceptions and egotism. Fathers assumed that they had the right to control sons, and sons thought they were the literal manifestation of Christ on the earth.

Horrible deformities of scriptural truth have paraded down the corridor of Church history. Nevertheless, the presence of abusive fathers and rebellious sons does not mean we abandon the righteous foundation of family and generational relationship in the Kingdom. The presence of counterfeits and frauds serves only to deepen our hunger for the real and genuine. A river might be polluted, but the crisp, clear creeks and sparkling streams that flow from the wellspring of its source should not be forsaken.

This book is intended to bring us into a tender relationship between fathers and sons that is the heart of the Kingdom. I pray that the ensuing pages of this volume prove to effect structural realignment in the Body of Christ and heal the weeping wounds of spiritual abuse by showing proper use of father authority and the honor of sons.

Introduction

As I reflect back, I now *realize* that this book began to be birthed many years ago during my pastoral Bible studies on the Book of Hebrews. I had been working through the fifth chapter over and over, emphasizing the importance and power of the priesthood of Christ. The focus of this particular course of study was to prepare the believer for ministry by observing the life of Jesus. Verses 12 through 14 of this chapter had really become my "bread and butter" Scriptures for showing the crying need for maturation in the believer and the absolute necessity for precise emulation:

> *For when for the time ye ought to be teachers, ye have need that one teach you again which be the first principles of the oracles of God; and are become such as have need of milk, and not of strong meat For every one that useth milk is unskillful in the word of righteousness: for he is a*

> ***babe. But strong meat belongeth to them that are of full age, even those who by reason of use have their senses exercised to discern both good and evil* (Hebrews 5:12-14).**

My presentation became fervent as I communicated this truth. To truly become the royal priesthood according to Peter's epistle (see 1 Pet. 2:9), we must find the proper pattern for spiritual induction into ministry. At this point I became aware of a truth that I had previously completely overlooked. With all the compounded information about the Melchisedec order, the prayers and supplications of Jesus, the obedience of a son and His authorship of eternal salvation, I had missed a simple yet powerful issue. Jesus had absolutely no right to ministry until His Father said, "Thou art My Son" (see Mk. 1:11). In other words, station of birth, gifts, skill, talent, ability, preparation, etc., mean nothing until a father voices his approval.

> ***And no man taketh this honour unto himself, but he that is called of God, as was Aaron. So also Christ glorified not Himself to be made an high priest; but He that said unto Him, Thou art My Son, today have I begotten Thee* (Hebrews 5:4-5).**

Having wandered upon this seemingly mute issue, I decided to test it against the hearts of my ministry peers and friends in various teachings and seminar-type settings. To my astonishment, the response was not only overwhelming, but also very discomfiting to me personally. As I closed my dissertations with Elisha crying, "My father, my father!"— complete with falling mantles and double portions, I was often surrounded by bewildered emotional men and women asking, "Dr. Hanby, would you consider being a covering for our work and ministry? We really don't have a father."

Equally unsettling to me was the number of others who rejoiced in telling me about their gospel father. They told me of the exact date and hour of their initial conversion, along with the name and background of the brother who had won them to the Lord. This, I believe, completely missed the point. The issue is not being sired into the Kingdom, but being fathered into ministry.

Another reaction that greatly dismayed me was hearing the names of seminaries, Bible schools, and correspondence materials from an array of well-known teachers in response to the necessity of father-son relationships. It really didn't help my concerns as letter after letter appeared on my desk requesting some kind of parental connection, often with folks whom I had never met or at least could not remember. Somewhere they had been in a meeting or had been handed a tape of some past message containing information about the necessary spiritual link between fathers and sons. The point of their correspondence was basically the same: "Would you be our father?"

Eventually I became comfortable with a personally patented answer. I offered it with great sincerity and conviction: "I really do not want to be anybody's daddy, but I will be a big brother or a best friend." I usually went on to say that I would freely and gladly furnish any information or materials at my disposal that might be a blessing to them and their ministries.

I also found a great deal of satisfaction in being

included in various presbyteries and peer ministry councils - especially since one of my chief foundational messages for years has been the "multiplicity of ministry." This message proposes and explains a compounded, multifaceted type of ministry, manifesting by that multiplicity a fuller expression of Christ. So then, rolling such terms as father, bishop, pastor, overseer, presbyter, etc. into one great summary title of "covering," I quite willingly accepted the more general title while shunning the more personal idea of fatherhood.

Then late this past summer I went into spiritual labor. I was sitting on my deck, drifting somewhere between jet lag and inspiration, meditating on the profound blessing of being home. My only distraction seemed to be captured in the line of some Old English poetry: "To mow or not to mow, that is the question." Other familiar literary passages encapsulated and expressed my deeper feelings: "Tomorrow and tomorrow and tomorrow." Then I felt pain, like a slow, certain aching in my spirit.

Eventually, I found myself wandering the all-too-familiar fields of burdened thought. These were not normal birth feelings that accompany new spiritual ideas, illumination, or revelation. Rather, they were a certain foreboding, a sense of the holy fear and respect that often goes before rebuke.

I felt caught away to the arid, lonely deserts where fell the bleached bones of countless thousands of misguided, purposeless, and failed ministries. This forlorn place lay lost between the springs of hopeful beginnings and the still waters of righteous consummation. The few who somehow managed to survive here packed practiced clichés and clutched cassette-canteens, sipping waters from stolen streams. It was in this wilderness of anguished recognition that the Lord began speaking to me.

At first I wrestled with what seemed to me to be several disconnected Scriptures lifted out of any certain context. As I continued to weigh them together, the meaning became clearer and clearer. One passage was Acts 17:30:

> ***And the times of this ignorance God winked at; but now commandeth all men everywhere to repent.***

The need for repentance dug deeply into my spirit and as I reached out for understanding, it became obvious to me that some out-of-order situation required attention and an eventual turnaround.

Then Malachi 4:5-6 dropped in on me and I knew I was in trouble:

> ***Behold, I will send you Elijah the prophet before the coming of the great and dreadful day of the Lord: and he shall turn the heart of the fathers to the children, and the heart of the children to their fathers, lest I come and smite the earth with a curse.***

There it was: "the heart of the fathers." That phrase shattered my peace and filled me with a painful remorse I hardly know how to express. The heart of this father had refused to be turned. I knew it did not mean that everyone who requested help automatically belonged to me. However, I was faced with the awful truth that some lonely, hurting men and women in gospel work had been rejected by me, thus leaving them either orphans or, even worse, bastards. Furthermore, any inheritance through either gifting or anointing was being withheld, causing them a painful endurance of spiritual wandering with single portions. Disconnected from anointing, the flow of purposeful ministry was interrupted. They were restricted to pouring forth life from their own vessels with only borrowed or stolen waters to replenish their supply. The result could only end in burnout and empty frustration.

Some who settle in to read the words of this book will immediately relate to those lonely sons while others will sense with me the pain of fatherly irresponsibility. If this introduction already seems too poignant and direct, then you will likely be offended by the following chapters, for they are truly the result of my deep repentance and search for absolute truth. Here you will see my heart laid bare and my soul unmasked. If you do choose to continue, you may also, with me and Malachi, determine to lift the curse and joyfully herald the coming of the spirit of Elijah.

Dr. Mark Hanby

"For though ye have ten thousand instructors in Christ, yet have ye not many fathers: for in Christ Jesus I have begotten you through the gospel."
1 Corinthians 4:15

Chapter 1

The Father's Dilemma

After the long ocean voyage, the young missionary fought his "sea legs" as he walked down the pier into a land far from home. The years of preparation, language study, and carrying the burden of prayer have finally found him at the shore of his dream. Full of passion for the lost and dying of this continent, the missionary yearned to share the love of Jesus with those who never heard His name. What the young man discovered was the religion of the American Church reached these people before the gospel of the Kingdom ever arrived.

The ministries that preceded his arrival served as beachhead operations for a denominational system on doctrinal stand instead of being heralds of God's Christ. As he passed building after building, the young minister noticed that each representative of the small Christian community here gathered under its own name: Anglican, Assembly of God, Baptist,

Presbyterian, Methodist, Church of Christ, Church of God, Independent, Fundamental, Apostolic, Primitive ... He wondered if each of these names served as a label of identity or simply marked the spot where these groups stopped in the progression of God's revelation.

"Is this what God is doing? Is this how Christ builds His Church? Or have we gone far astray of our purpose and design, becoming the very world we are trying to turn toward Jesus? Where have we gone wrong and how can we return to a simplicity in Christ? These and other thoughts ran through the missionary's mind, but in the busyness of his day with so many things to do for God, he let those questions rest. Such issues as these distract a person from programs and parades, from meetings and money-counting, from form and functions. Yet, late that night, after settling in for a length stay, the young man hungered in his heart for reality in God.

The Father's Dilemma

Rarely has a church received more from God than the people of early Corinth did. First planted in foundational truth by the apostle Paul, the Corinthians were then watered by the eloquent flow of scriptural insight from Apollos. Later they would be enriched by the testimony of the greatest living eyewitness to the ministry of Jesus in that day, the apostle Peter. Corinth was indeed favored of the Lord. The church was full of the Word, and the abundance of spiritual gifting in Corinth seems unparalleled even by New Testament standards. Considering the great wealth of revelation, insight, and charismatic expression that was deposited in this early Christian community, it would seem right to consider this setting as a model of all that the Church should become. However, even a casual reading in our Bibles of the Corinthian correspondence reveals not a model, but a mess.

According to Paul's writings, the Corinthians were a fellowship of factions and fornicators. A congregation of carnal charismatics, their gatherings were egotistical exhibitions of spiritual gifts. A diagnosis of the Body of Christ at Corinth would use such terms as disunity, dysfunction, and disorder. Their ignorant use of their gifting was a symptom of a confusion concerning their identity. The Corinthians did not base their identity on who they were in Christ. Instead, they sought to establish their identity by gathering themselves under the name of a famous preacher. They said "I am of Paul, and I of

Apollos, and I of Cephas, and I of Christ." By joining themselves to a well-known name, they gained a mark of identity and an elevated sense of importance that was not of God.

The Corinthians also sought their identity through whatever gift of the Spirit that was demonstrated in their lives. Just as they elevated their favorite preacher above any other preacher, so the many members of the Corinthian church elevated their personal gifting as the source of their identity. Evidently many of the Corinthian Christians prophesied or spoke in tongues and felt not only that their gift was greater than that of others, but also that they themselves were "more excellent" because of their gifting! Their use of charismatic gifts as a mark of identity instead of as ministry to the Body caused the confusion and indecency present within their congregational gatherings. It is into this setting that Paul wrote the following words:

> **I *write not these things to shame you, but as my beloved sons I warn you. For though ye have ten thousand instructors in Christ, yet have ye not many fathers: for in Christ Jesus I have begotten you through the gospel. Wherefore I beseech you, be ye followers of me. For this cause have I sent unto you Timotheus, who is my beloved son, and faithful in the Lord, who shall bring you into remembrance of my ways which be in Christ, as I teach everywhere in every church* (1 Corinthians 4:14-17).**

In these few sentences the apostle shows the Corinthian church the way out of their dilemma. Paul reminds them to become his followers, since he is their father in the gospel. He speaks to them as sons and is sending his son in the

Lord, Timothy, to bring them into remembrance-to remember them-into apostolic truth. The apostle Paul is not on some ego trip to spiritual stardom by pleading with a group of Christians to become his followers. Paul is well aware of his own identity, saying later in this same letter:

> *For I am the least of the apostles, that am not meet to be called an apostle, because I persecuted the church of God. But by the grace of God I am what I am: and His grace which was bestowed upon me was not in vain; but I laboured more abundantly than they all: yet not I, but the grace of God which was with me (1* **Corinthians 15:9-10).**

Paul knew who he was and why he was given his place in God. It was the Corinthian church that was not receiving Paul's fatherhood and had no true father to follow. As long as a congregation or ministry stays out of God's order, the people will have disorder and lack identity. If we are without a father, then we have no name, no identity, no heritage, no inheritance, and no true brethren.

The order of God within His Kingdom is the order of father and son. Paul writes to a chaotic charismatic culture as a father to sons and sends Timothy as a model of what a son in the ministry is really like. The apostle then says that this is part of Paul's "ways which be in Christ, as I teach everywhere in every church." If we are ever going to find our way out of this confusion, we have to find God's ways in the Kingdom.

We must return to God's principle of father and son. This truth was lost in the Church because we modeled our relationships according to modern practices of business management instead of following a biblical pattern. We hire pastors and leaders to perform certain functions within an organizational structure that mirrors the operation of a chicken or hamburger franchise more than it reflects spiritual truth.

Today a local church will associate with a large ministry or its denominational headquarters and serve as a franchise representative of that well-known product line. The local church receives its name, its logo, and its organizational security by attaching itself to a nationally known "chain." Pastors become CEO's of these locally run outposts that hire assistant managers to perform in specific areas: visitation, music, youth, office administration, etc. The pastor, along with his assistants, help to recruit and train a volunteer staff to perform programmed tasks. This results in more business and recruitment of new customers who support more buildings at better locations. We call this church growth. We call this success. But what does God call it?

We do things God never told us to do. God never told us to form ourselves like the nations of the world. He never said to develop systems that divide truth into separate camps by naming and numbering the people. We made our denominations so we could appear like all the other nations. The organizations of God's Kingdom should be modeled after His Word, not the principles of this world. The Church is more than a franchise on the street corner; it is more than a preacher's union. The Church is to be the representative of Kingdom truth in the earth.

Our relationships in ministry are based on a voting process of majority rule instead of on God's rulership. Authority flows from "headquarters," a disconnected part of headship that substitutes politics and organizational authority for familial dependence. The covering of ministry has become a legal facade, not a true garment for a priest. Men want respectability, and they want their own name. Good men and women of God are placed in positions as pastors and leaders of fellowships, and then are removed by the same dictates of carnal leadership systems. The will of the Lord becomes secondary to the dictates of men.

Those who know that denominations are not the answer form "fellowships" and call themselves "non-denominational," or "independent." By calling themselves these names, they feel covered enough to commit the same practices, sometimes with even more corruption than the very system that they left. Shakespeare wrote, "A rose by any other name still smells as sweet." A system that follows worldly principles of power and relationship is still of the world, regardless of official position or title.

Because the Church has not followed the ways of her Redeemer, non-biblical relationships have produced a non-biblical generation. God does not call us just His "ambassadors" or His "ministers." He calls us His children, His sons, the church of the Firstborn, His Bride, and His Body! We have built ministry relationships based on the kingdom of this world, not on the Kingdom of our God and His Christ! That is why we are great at building churches, but not at participating in true Kingdom experience. Our enormous numerical growth is dwarfed by the power of 120 men and women in the upper room. The purpose of the Church is to be an outpost for the Kingdom, not a man-made, man-patterned, and institutional, bloodless machine that produces programs and numbers, but not sons and daughters.

When God's people refuse to follow His order, the judgment they receive is a lack of any order and a loss of truth and revelation. When the excellency of God's Word is not applied to the Church, then the excellence that comes from God is removed from the Church. The prophet Isaiah writes:

> *For, behold, the Lord, the Lord of hosts, doth take away from Jerusalem and from Judah the stay and the staff, the whole stay of bread, and the whole stay of water. The mighty man, and the man of war, the judge, and the prophet, and the prudent, and the ancient, the captain of fifty, and the honourable man, and the counsellor, and the cunning artificer, and the eloquent orator* **(Isaiah 3:1-3).**

This prophecy reflects the situation in 606 B.C. when Nebuchadnezzar took all the treasure and best people from Judah into Babylon. For instance, the prophet Daniel and his three friends were some of the princes and mighty men who were removed as leaders from Israel at that time (see 2 Kings 24:13-16). Because of Israel's sin, the Lord removed excellence from the supply of leadership as a judgment to turn the remnant from going into further transgression and deeper judgment. God will always remove the best in order to bring the rest into alignment with His purpose.

Where is the power of God in the Church today? Where are the mighty men, the apostles and prophets of yore who spoke and nations trembled? God has taken away His excellence from us so that we will return to His ways. God desires to fully restore the Church to the Kingdom. "He taketh away the first, that he may establish the second" (Heb. 10:9b). God takes away mature leadership, which results in the loss of excellence in leadership:

> ***And I will give children to be their princes, and babes shall rule over them. And the people shall be oppressed, everyone by another, and every one by his neighbor: the child shall behave himself proudly against the ancient, and the base against the honourable*** **(Isaiah 3:4-5).**

When the people of God refuse maturity in Christ, they are judged by losing maturity and having immature individuals in leadership positions. The fathers are replaced with children.

When Paul tells the Corinthians that they have "ten thousand instructors in Christ, yet have ye not many fathers" (1 Cor. 4:15), he is referring to the root of their problem: a lack of mature father leadership. Instead of having many fathers, they had ten thousand instructors. The word for "instructor" here in the Greek is *paidagogos,* which means "boy-leader." This term refers to a servant whose official position was to make sure the children went to school. Thus fathers were substituted by hired servants, unrelated to spiritual inheritance.

Today there are thousands of ministry people who have been educated in the finest schools. Many have supplemented their formal education through audiotapes and videotapes as well as through books and magazines from qualified scholarly sources. Although there has never been a greater flood of biblical material available there are precious few drops of biblical power manifested. We reach millions with information, but without spiritual relationship, impartational truth is not given and received.

The reason we have not seen a manifestation of power in biblical proportions is because we are not giving and receiving impartation by the biblical pattern. We have ten thousand "boy-leaders" in Christ, but not many fathers.

One of the results of a fatherless church is oppression. Isaiah said, "And the people shall be oppressed, everyone by another, and every one by his neighbor: the child shall behave himself proudly against the ancient, and the base against the honorable" (Is. 3:5).

A family without a father suffers financially, socially, and psychologically, as well as spiritually. The pressure on single mothers and fatherless children is oppressive. When a father is not present in a home to train the children in matters of the Lord, the hearts of the children turn to rage and they dishonor authority (see Eph. 6:14). Oppression occurs when immature rulers serve as baby-sitters over congregations, leading the people without having any true vision. "Where there is no vision, the people perish" (Prov. 29:18a).

Another trait of a fatherless church is the desire for an identity. Isaiah writes:

> *When a man shall take hold of his brother of the house of his father, saying, Thou hast clothing, be thou our ruler, and let this ruin be under thy hand: In that day shall he swear, saying, I will not be an healer; for in my house is neither bread nor clothing: make me not a ruler of the people. ...And*

> *in that day seven women shall take hold of one man, saying, We will eat our own bread, and wear our own apparel: only let us be called by thy name, to take away our reproach* **(Isaiah 3:6-7; 4:1).**

The Israelites grabbed hold of anyone they thought looked good enough to be their leader. The right clothes and appearance were the only qualification for leadership. If the person dressed for success, then he was a success. The shortage of fathers made gender alone the qualification to be the head of a house.

With a lack of fathers comes a lack of identity. We need so desperately to belong, to have boundaries, to know who we are in God. An orphan will seek for many years for any information he can find concerning his heritage, for without a family line he will never really know himself. He may have many brothers and sisters, but without any knowledge of his father, he will never be able to recognize their kinship. Perhaps he is the recipient of a large inheritance, yet without proof of his lineage, he will never be qualified to receive it.

Many Christian leaders today can, when questioned, give a list of men whose teaching influenced their lives, but these same leaders cannot point to a father in the ministry. Thus, like the Corinthian church, we have ample instruction and abundant gifting, but we have not many fathers. As a result, we gather under the banner of a particular teacher or organization for our identity. Or we use our particular gifting as our source of personhood in the Kingdom, which perverts the very purpose of the gifts God gave to men. The product of this disorder is a sick, infantile Church. Unable to walk in the Spirit, she totters and sways, fulfilling the lusts of her flesh.

What the Church must have is a renewal, not only of the Holy Spirit, but also of relational patterns in ministry. We must rediscover the wonderful truth of impartational relationship in the order of father to son. When we find God's order, we will know our identity and fulfill our purpose in the Kingdom of God.

And no man taketh this honour unto himself, but he that is called of God, as was Aaron. So also Christ glorified not Himself to be made an high priest; but He that said unto Him, Thou art My Son, to day have I begotten Thee.

Hebrews 5:4-5

Chapter 2

The Father's Order

"Order in the court!" The judge demanded the composure of the courtroom with an authority that was absolute. He maintained structure with the skill of a surgeon so that the operation of justice could continue undisturbed. A child offender, a juvenile delinquent, stood before him. Little could be said in this case; the young man was undeniably guilty. He did not present any arguments. His only plea was for the court to show mercy.

The father is present, but not close. He appeared only in an attempt to bail his son out of trouble again. He hoped that with a checkbook and pen, he could pay for his son's mistake. But the judge was not interested in his money. Instead he asked for an account of where the father was while his child grew up.

The father responded with a brief history of his own childhood. By the time he was born, his father had already left the family. He had to abandon his childhood to be the "man of the house". Working hard for little pay, he cursed the father he never knew for the poverty he knew too well, and vowed that his son would never be poor. Standing in the courtroom, he admitted that in his efforts to make a better life for his family, he rarely had time for fatherhood. But he pointed out the fact that he had afforded his son every luxury.

However, when the judge looked down from his bench, he saw an impoverished child with a lot of money whose crime was theft. He broke the law in an attempt to steal his father's attention. How should the court rule in such a case? The judge had compassion, but he knew the danger of leniency, where loopholes become vicious cycles that never end. He reasoned that it was better to use a bit of discomfort with a tight rein on mercy to lead this young man into maturity.

The defendant was found guilty and his father was held responsible. The sentence given the son was 40 hours of community service to learn how to earn honor and respect. The father was requested to pay a generous amount of attention to his son to learn the value of relationship.

The gavel hit the bench the same way a hammer hit a nail into a sure place. The court had made its decision in favor of the future and condemned a dysfunctional past. Justice was served and relationships were secured by a judge who brought order into the court of father and son.

The Father's Order

In the beginning, the order of the universe was perfection. From the smallest flower to the highest flying bird, everything was in harmony—including relationships. But when sin entered the world, this natural order of perfection became chaos. Instead of perfection reproducing perfection, thorns began to grow and choke perfection out.

Weeds and disease began to spread as animal began to prey on animal, locked into a shackle of sin called a food chain. Chaos was producing chaos. The perfection that was once natural, now took effort to keep. In the same way, our relationships require work. Just as we must pull up weeds, so we must pull up roots of bitterness and learn to not devour one another.

We must begin again and learn how to sow into the lives of others in order to reap the harvest of righteous relationships. We begin with the order of father and son.

It was through the relationship of father and son that God intervened and promised a Savior through the righteous seed of Seth. "And I will put enmity between thee and the woman, and between thy seed and her seed; it shall bruise thy head, and thou shalt bruise his heel" (Gen. 3:15).

Nine generations after Adam, we find God's heart turned against His children because of their wickedness. "And God saw that the wickedness of man was great in the earth, and that every imagination of the thoughts of his heart was only evil continually. And it repented the Lord that He had made man on the earth, and it grieved Him at His heart." (Gen. 6:5-6).

This would have been the end of the sons of Adam, except that "Noah found grace in the eyes of the Lord." (Gen. 6:8). God found a son He could make a father. The Lord saved Noah, his wife, his sons, and their wives. They were all saved because they were of the house of their father, Noah. Noah became a father to the human race, and a father in ministry, when he offered a sacrifice upon their disembarkment from the ark.

God would later bless a man named Abram, the son of Terah, the son of Shem, the son of Noah. God raised this man to be a father of a nation, "For I know him that he will command his children and his household after him, and they shall keep the way of the Lord" (Gen. 18:19a).

From Abraham would come Isaac, Jacob, and 12 sons: 12 tribes, one nation. Abraham, Isaac, and Jacob were all fathers in the ministry and fathers to a nation. Each of Jacob's sons were fathers to a tribe. The blessing of God passed from father to son.

Seventy-five people went down into Egypt and millions came out. When Israel was in bondage to Egypt, God's heart turned toward His children. God looked upon the entire nation as His son. All the firstborn of Egypt would die and Israel go free because "...Thus saith the Lord, Israel is My son, even My firstborn" (Ex. 4:22). This nation would be delivered by God through a father in the ministry named Moses.

Although God chose to give promises to all the children of Abraham, He chose only one tribe to serve in His house.

The Father's Order

The tabernacle was to be manned and its services performed by one tribe: the tribe of Levi. Out of the Levites, one family, the line of Aaron, was chosen to serve as priests entering into the Holy Place. Aaron was established as the father to the priesthood by Moses. The priesthood also was in the order of father to son.

And take thou unto thee Aaron thy brother, and his sons with him, from among the children of Israel, that he may minister unto Me in the priest's office, even Aaron, Nadab and Abihu, Eleazar and Ithamar, Aaron's sons (**Exodus 28:1**).

And thou shalt bring Aaron and his sons unto the door of the tabernacle of the congregation, and wash them with water. And thou shalt put upon Aaron the holy garments, and anoint him, and sanctify him; that he may minister unto Me in the priest's office. And thou shalt bring his sons, and clothe them with coats: and thou shalt anoint them, as thou didst anoint their father, that they may minister unto Me in the priest's office: for their anointing shall surely be an everlasting priesthood throughout their generations (**Exodus 40:12-15**).

Aaron and his four sons serve as a shadow of the fivefold ministry gifts in the Church: "And He gave some, apostles; and some, prophets; and some, evangelists; and some, pastors and teachers" (Eph. 4:11). Though all the Israelites were children of Abraham and worshipers of Jehovah, only Aaron and his generations after him could minister in the office of a priest. Talent, intelligence, education, dedication, and desire for the Lord are wonderful attributes in God's family, but they are never qualifications for ministry. The only everlasting priesthood is *throughout their generations.* To be a priest, your father must be a priest.

Not only were the offices of high priest and priest filled in the order of father to son, but the diaconate of the Old Testament, the Levites, were also chosen in the same order: "And thy brethren also of the tribe of Levi, the tribe of thy father, bring thou with thee, that they may be joined unto thee, and minister unto thee: but thou and thy sons with thee shall minister before the tabernacle of witness" (Num. 18:2).

The sons of Levi served unto the sons of Aaron. From playing music to moving furniture, the Levites served as helpers and assistants to the priests. No matter how menial the labor may have seemed, the work was considered true ministry. Therefore, because the Levites were ministers, the basis of qualification for their ministry was being a son of Levi. Just as Aaron had to be your father for you to be a priest, you could not even dump the ashes from the brazen altar unless your father was a Levite.

All mankind has sinned and fallen short of the glory of God because of their father, Adam. The salvation of the human race at the Flood was by one father: Noah. All the people of Israel were chosen by God from one father: Abraham. All the priests were from one father: Aaron. All the Levites were from one father: Levi. Everything in God is from father to son. Any departure from God's order is a departure from God.

This order was perverted in the days of Eli the high priest. The light of the priesthood became darkened when Eli's sons, Hophni and Phineas (called by God the sons of Belial), stole from the offerings and used their office to have

The Father's Order

illicit sexual relationships. Then these false priests faced a battle with the Philistines. They thought that if the Ark of the Covenant was paraded before the army as they went into battle, they would surely be victorious.

Merely parading a covenant not kept is not the secret of victory. The Lord invites His people not only to power, but also to relationship. Eli and his sons died on the same day they carried the Ark. At the same time, the line of Eli gave birth to "Ichabod." They produced "no glory." The family line of Eli ended there.

However, God had already provided a way to preserve the order of father to son. God answered the prayer of a woman named Hannah, who gave her firstborn son into the service of the house of God. God called Samuel to be the new father to Israel, to be "a faithful priest, that shall do according to that which is in Mine heart and in My mind: and I will build him a sure house; and he shall walk before Mine anointed forever" (1 Sam. 2:35). Samuel was a transitional man in the progression of God's people toward their ultimate purpose of bringing forth a Messiah. He would be a bridge between the rejection of one line of a father's house and the prophet who established the line of the Messiah.

Samuel's sons were to follow him in ministry. However...

And it came to pass, when Samuel was old, that he made his sons judges over Israel. ... And his sons walked not in his ways, but turned aside after lucre, and took bribes, and perverted judgment. Then all the elders of Israel gathered themselves together, and came to Samuel unto Ramah, and said unto him, Behold, thou art old, and thy sons walk not in thy ways: now make us a king to judge us like all the nations. But the thing displeased Samuel, when they said, Give us a king to judge us. And Samuel prayed unto the Lord. **(1 Samuel 8:1, 3-6).**

Samuel's sons were "turned aside after lucre, and took bribes, and perverted judgment" (1 Sam. 8:3). Their hearts were turned to their flesh, not toward their father. This time the Israelite leadership was not willing to trust God to fix the corrupt situation as He did in Eli's case. Instead of praying for revival within God's order, the people changed the order of God for the order of man. Their desire to be as other nations was greater than their trust in God. The wounding of their past caused them to not trust the order of God any longer.

The sons of Samuel were definitely corrupt. They were not fit to rule the people of God. Corrupt rulership does not mean we abandon the order of father and son, however. To abandon the order of God is to be just as unrighteous as the leaders themselves. Unwillingness to submit to God's order is unwillingness to submit to God. The correct response in this situation is to pray for the restoration of righteousness within the order of God. Prayer out of a barren situation brought Samuel to lead the people of God. If they had prayed, God would have sent a new order of father and son in ministry.

When the people desired to be like the other nations and follow a king instead of follow God, they lost the flow of generational blessing that is passed from father to son. By changing the form of their submission, they not only rejected the order of God, they also cut themselves off from the blessing contained within the order they rejected.

The Father's Order

> *Then all the elders of Israel gathered themselves together, and came to Samuel unto Ramah, and said unto him, Behold, thou art old, and thy sons walk not in thy ways: now make us a king to judge us like all the nations* **(1 Samuel 8:4-5).**

The establishment of the kingdom of man was based on the rejection of the order of fathers and sons. This was a rejection of God Himself.

> *And the Lord said unto Samuel, Hearken unto the voice of the people in all that they say unto thee: for they have not rejected thee, but they have rejected Me, that I should not reign over them. According to all the works which they have done since the day that I brought them up out of Egypt even unto this day, wherewith they have forsaken Me, and served other gods, so do they also unto thee. Now therefore hearken unto their voice: howbeit yet protest solemnly unto them, and shew them the manner of the king that shall reign over them* **(1 Samuel 8:7-9).**

Samuel described what being like the other nations would be like. He described what systems of men do to the people of God. "And Samuel told all the words of the Lord unto the people that asked of him a king. And he said, This will be the manner of the king that shall reign over you..."

"He will take your sons, and appoint them for himself."

"He will set them to ear [plow] his ground, and to reap his harvest."

"He will set them to make his instruments of war, and instruments of his chariots."

"He will take your daughters to be confectionaries, and to be cooks, and to be bakers."

"He will take your fields, and your vineyards, and your oliveyards, even the best of them, and give them to his servants."

"He will take the tenth of your seed, and of your vineyards, and give to his officers, and to his servants."

"He will take your menservants, your maidservants, and your goodliest young men, and put them to his work."

"He will take the tenth of your sheep, and ye shall be his servants."

"And ye shall cry out in that day because of your king which ye shall have chosen you; and the Lord will not hear you in that day." (See 1 Samuel 8:10-18.)

The people rejected Samuel's warning. They rejected God's order for the system of man.

"Nevertheless the people refused to obey the voice of Samuel; and they said, Nay; but we will have a king over us; that we also may be like all the nations; and that our king may judge us, and go out before us, and fight our battles" (1 Sam. 8:19-20). Because the people of God wanted to have a king like all the other nations, Samuel anointed Saul to be the first king of Israel. Saul was also given Samuel as a father in the ministry (see 1 Sam. 10:12).

Saul's heart did not stay toward his ministry father, though. Saul disobeyed the Lord twice. Both times Saul's disobedience was based on his attempt to follow the demands of men when he was anointed to follow the Lord.

The Father's Order

"Then came the word of the Lord unto Samuel, saying, It repenteth Me that I have set up Saul to be king: for he is turned back from following Me, and hath not performed My commandments..." (1 Sam. 15:10-11). Because Saul's heart would not be turned, God's heart was turned (He repented) from having Saul as king.

To replace Saul, God looks past six brothers, all kingly in their appearance, to find a man after His own heart. A shepherd boy will become king.

David was anointed as king. David would fight valiantly, rule graciously, and sin horribly. But when he falls, David seeks the renewal of heart and spirit that are available to those who are turned toward the father.

It is David who will desire to build God a house. However, God told David that He never told him or anyone else to build Him a house. Instead, God is the One who will build David a house—a house that will be established forever. When the temple stones are dust, the house of David will still flourish! This house will be through the order of father and son; David's son will sit upon the throne forever. God adopts David as His firstborn son, and the house of David as His own.

> *.. Also the Lord telleth thee that He will make thee an house. And when thy days be fulfilled, and thou shalt sleep with thy fathers, I will set up thy seed after thee, which shall proceed out of thy bowels, and I will establish his kingdom. ... I will be his father, and he shall be My son. If he commit iniquity, I will chasten him with the rod of men, and with the stripes of the children of men: but My mercy shall not depart away from*

***him, as I took it from Saul, whom I put away before thee* (2 Samuel 7:11-15).**

God never wanted His people to be under the kingdom of man, but under the kingdom of God. Men were placed as kings by God because people rejected His ways. The order of father and son is not simply one theme among many in Scripture; it is the foundational principle for all spiritual understanding in the Kingdom.

When God chose to fully manifest Himself, He followed the order of father and son. "God, who at sundry times and in divers manners spake in time past unto the fathers by the prophets, hath in these last days spoken unto us by his Son..." (Heb. 1:1-2). Jesus did nothing outside the perfect fulfillment of the order of father to son.

The Son of God walked in the order of father and son while on earth. Jesus, though Deity incarnate, did not exercise divine power unless directed so by the Father. He who calmed the seas, drove out devils, and rose from the dead said, "The Son can do nothing of Himself, but what He seeth the Father do" (Jn. 5:19b). Jesus came into the world, sent by the Father. He spoke to us the words of His Father, did the works of His Father, was crucified in obedience to the will of the Father, and was raised again and ascended to the Father! Jesus did not perform any ministry act until the pattern of father to son was fulfilled at the River Jordan.

The Lord Jesus, in whom God was manifest in the flesh, did not initiate His ministry until He was declared to be the Son of the Father: "And no man taketh this honor unto himself, but he that is called of God, as was Aaron. So also Christ glorified not Himself to be made an high priest; but He that

The Father's Order

said unto Him, Thou art My Son, today have I begotten Thee" (Heb. 5:4-5).

We may have had many teachers and instructors. We may have been taught by a dozen different professors in the seminary, but we do not have many fathers. Jesus Himself, the supreme example of all Christian ministry, did not execute a single ministry act except as a son to a father. If Jesus did not minister outside the order of father and son, then we have no right to ministry if we do not follow the same order.

The flow of ministry always proceeds from father to son. When Elijah departed in a fiery chariot, Elisha did not cry out "My prophet" or "My teacher." He cried, "My father, my father" (2 Kings 2:12). When the apostle Paul wrote to Timothy or Titus, he did not write "my assistant" or "my student" but "my own son in the faith" (1 Tim. 1:2). Without the spiritual relationship of father to son, there can never be the passing of double portions or a true basis of spiritual authority and identity.

The order of father and son is the basis of all ministry in both the Old and New Testaments. Paul, in writing to Timothy, says, "Unto Timothy, my own son in the faith" (1 Tim. 1:2) and "Thou therefore, my son, be strong in the grace that is in Christ Jesus" (2 Tim. 2:1). The people of God are one family in the spiritual realm, and the link between father and son in ministry is not physical either. Timothy was not the natural son of Paul. The order of ministry according to the Word of God is always father to son, but it is an order of the Spirit and does not require natural generation. Consider these examples:

The impartation from Moses, the man of God, to

Joshua (Num. 27:15-20; Deut. 34:9).

The anointing from the prophet Samuel to Saul (1 Sam. 10:12).

The anointing from the prophet Samuel to David (1 Sam 16:13).

The transfer of prophetic mantles from Elijah to Elisha (2 Kings 2:12).

The relationship of Paul and Titus (Tit 1:4).

The connection between a son and a father in ministry has always been one of the Spirit.

The whole key to this order is the passing of generational blessing and inheritance from father to son. It is in the order of father to son that spiritual impartation occurs. By the laying on of hands the apostle Paul deposited a spiritual endowment unto Timothy, his son: "Wherefore I put thee in remembrance that thou stir up the gift of God, which is in thee by the putting on of my hands" (2 Tim. 1:6).

This is the special order of passing spiritual impartation in ministry: father to son. When a father lays his hands upon a son, it is not for the mere transmission of thoughts and ideas. It is an impartation of spirit. When this impartation occurs, a man pours his spiritual genetic code, his vision and his burden, into the heart of his kneeling son.

The order of God has not changed through the entire history of relationship with man. God established the order of natural life to flow from father to son. God based all spiritual inheritance upon the order of father to son in ministry. Adam, as father to all men, passed his unrighteous condition to all men. Noah became the new father to mankind after the flood. Abraham was the father and head of a physical and spiritual dynasty. He brings us all the other fathers in ministry: Moses, Aaron, Levi, Joshua, Samuel, Saul, David, and Jesus, the Son of David.

Everything we have in God comes from a father-to-son relationship. Gleaming like stars in the winter night, biblical phrases abound, like "tribe of thy father"; "blessing of thy father"; "house of thy father"; "iniquity of their fathers"; "inheritance of the fathers"; "promise to the fathers"; and "God of thy fathers." Even when a man dies, he is "gathered unto his fathers," or "slept with his fathers."

We are the result of the order of God of father to son. This is the order of our salvation. This is the order of the ministry. This is the Kingdom of God.

Samuel showed the people of God what happens when the ways of God are rejected and replaced with the ways of men.

> *Now therefore stand and see this great thing, which the Lord will do before your eyes. Is it not wheat harvest to day? I will call unto the Lord, and He shall send thunder and rain; that ye may perceive and see that your wickedness is great, which ye have done in the sight of the Lord, in asking you a king* **(1 Samuel 12:16-17).**

The harvest was destroyed because the kingdom of man was substituted for the Kingdom of God. When the Church rejects the revelation of God and establishes her own kingdom instead of His, the result is devastation of the harvest.

The people of this world are crying out to know the God who created them. But the only way they will ever know the Father is through the Son. The way the world will see Jesus is through the order of father and son manifested in the Church. The whole creation groans and travails in pain together until now, waiting for the manifestation of the sons of God. (see Rom. 8:19,22).

Unless the fathers and sons turn toward each other, God will smite the earth with a curse, as Malachi prophesied.

And the Lord thy God will bring thee into the land which thy fathers possessed, and thou shalt possess it; and He will do thee good, and multiply thee above thy fathers.
— Deuteronomy 30:5

Chapter 3

The Father's Inheritance

Sitting at the glass-covered, highly polished desk, the pastor prepared for his Sunday morning message. Saturdays were always confusing. Nevertheless he must complete his preparation today. He must be ready; so much depends on his leadership.

When glancing around this pastor's well-appointed office, it is hard to miss the finely framed parchments. These are the sealed documents with large, fancy signatures announcing his theological accomplishments, complete with organizational licenses and honorary presentations. The commendation letters from the city fathers are among his favorites.

Somewhat distracted, he reflected with mixed emotion on the past week's activities. Monday was staff meeting. Something still had to be done about the mishandling of calls, and without doubt confrontation concerning tardiness and lack of commitment was inevitable.

Tuesday he spent the entire day in counseling sessions and visitation. His children were upset because he had missed their recital but "God's work comes first." He had tried to help them understand. Of course Wednesday was spent mostly in preparation for the evening Bible study, interrupted several times by phone calls and call backs.

Thursday was correspondence day ... by the way, he had forgotten the letter of recommendation for the jail ministry team. Reaching for a pad, he jotted down a few notes. He paused in the middle of his writing, remembering the Friday evening fiasco. She just did not understand.

He should have been at home working on this message then, but his wife had insisted they go out together for dinner. She was irritated, commenting that he was inattentive and non-conversational. Explanations about the weekend responsibilities and church situations did little to comfort her. She just wanted some quality time alone and had added cynically, "I might as well be alone."

Although the words wisely did not pass his lips, he had mentally protested, "If you had to preach Sunday, you would not be acting this way!" She had gone to bed without speaking.

It was already two o'clock and his son had pleaded for his attendance at the Little League opener at five. "Three hours ... I have to hurry!"

Like a general anticipating the next day's battle, the pastor pondered his strategy. With waning numerical growth, the message should probably be evangelistic. However, the constant restlessness and criticism of the congregation pulled his mind toward the idea of unity and cordial response. It would be wonderful if the message were interrupted by response... He needed something unusual something very powerful!

Scanning his bulging bookshelves he usually browsed past Spurgeon, Foger, Wiersbe, Ford's Simple Sermon Outlines, Pulpit Helps, Wesley, Finney ... Sometimes the old can be new. With his power of presentation, he could make it work.

Wait, what was that new one about darkness and spirits ... spirits ... maybe angels. Dear God, if he could just see one right then!

The rapture! That could go both ways. The saints are eager to get out of here and the sinners are scared they will miss it!

Fumbling through the pile of already scrutinized ministry magazines he mused, "Nothing really hot here."

Glancing toward the credenza, he spied the tape. Snapping it in, he hit the play button and leaned back, listening thoughtfully to the introduction to the conference message. His associate had been really take by it and highly recommended that he hear it ... "Wow, that's powerful! Who is this guy?"

Pencil in hand, lead, letters, and borrowed phrases cover the face of the yellow pad, forming the outline. He is ready! "Now where did I put the car keys?"

With stolen assurance and justified hypocrisy, the pastor reminded himself that everyone gets their stuff from somewhere. He further comforted himself with the idea that *"nobody has a corner n God"* or a copyright on inspiration.

The time came. Mounting the platform, he smiled charismatically at the waiting congregation and began speaking with the familiar prophetic intonation. *"Yesterday I was in my study in prayer and God spoke to me ..."*

The Father's Inheritance

One of the basic premises of this book is that the blessing of generations has been lost to today's Church. In the Bible, the present generation was to receive the promises of the previous generations through the fathers. The "God of Abraham" became "the God of Abraham and the God of Isaac." Then He became "the God of Abraham, Isaac, and Jacob." The revelation of God grows through the generations.

The Bible is a book recorded for the generations. "This shall be written for the generation to come: and the people which shall be created shall praise the Lord" (Ps. 102:18; "One generation shall praise Thy works to another, and shall declare Thy mighty acts" (Ps. 145:4). The very purpose of the written Bible is so we would receive God. It is not in a single revelation, but through a written record of the rich inheritance of generational relationship.

We today tend to gingerly skip over all the lists of "begats" in the Scriptures. All those details of the generations of Adam, Noah, Shem, Terah, Jacob, and the 12 tribes of Israel, we sometimes feel are not essential. Although these genealogical lists may seem irrelevant to us, it is imperative we understand that the very presence of these large lists, repeated over and over in our Bibles, indicates an enormous generational interest in the heart of God.

The New Testament begins in Matthew's Gospel with the genealogy of Jesus. This demonstrates that the foundation of the New Testament revelation is in the generations that preceded Christ. In the Gospel of Luke the genealogy of Jesus is placed not at His birth, but at the inception of His ministry. Thus Matthew shows that the life of Jesus is based on previous generations, and Luke demonstrates that the genealogy of Jesus has direct bearing on His ministry. Just as Jesus cannot be born without a family, so Jesus cannot minister without a record of His ancestry (see Ezra 2:62).

Receiving our inheritance depends upon the flow of impartation and blessing from generation to generation in the family of God. Abraham was chosen as the father of the faith because God could say this of him: "For I know him that he will command his children and his household after him, and they shall keep the way of the Lord" (Gen. 18:19).

Abraham has one son of promise from a barren situation. He is wealthy by the standards of his day and lives a full life. Yet even though Abraham was promised the land that he sojourned in, he himself would only own a small burial plot and a few wells. (See Acts 7:5.)

His son Isaac would also have two sons from a barren situation. The birth of twins here is significant because it is a sign of double-portion blessing by the process of spiritual generation. It is the increase of generations in God.

The next generational increase is in the life of Jacob. He has two children from the barrenness of Rachel, and ten other children from Leah and two concubines. From 1 to 2 to 12, the increase of God can expand from generation to generation (see Deut. 32:30).

After Jacob, the 12 sons become 12 tribes. A nation of millions returned to Canaan in power and strength.

The Father's Inheritance

Though their numerical increase was great, their blessing was greater. The seed of Abraham was rich beyond compare, and instead of a little cave and a few springs, the nation of Israel received the entirety of the land. The children of a man who lived in a tent now inhabited cities they did not build. They ate crops they did not cultivate and fruit from trees they did not plant, and drank wine from vines they did not grow. They had cattle they did not raise and they drank from wells they did not dig. They received all this because they were sons to a father.

They not only increased physically, financially, and socially, but also spiritually. Abraham, their father, waited to hear the voice of God through lonely vigils and dark nights. His seed had written the law of Moses. Abraham sacrificed his own lambs, but his children had an established priesthood. The father worshiped under stars, not knowing exactly where God could be found. His sons had a house of God: "And there I will meet with the children of Israel, and the tabernacle shall be sanctified by My glory" (Ex. 29:43).

Abraham knows God by "El Shaddai," but his children called Him "Yahweh." "And I appeared unto Abraham, unto Isaac, and unto Jacob, by the name of God Almighty, but by My name JEHOVAH was I not known to them" (Ex. 6:3).

This is the progression of spiritual generation that begins in a single stream, but flows into a mighty ocean. This is the magnification of the blessing of God as it is transferred by spiritual inheritance from father to son.

The danger lies in that we are only one generation from

losing everything we have in God: "And also all that generation were gathered unto their fathers: and there arose another generation after them, which knew not the Lord, nor yet the works which He had done for Israel" (Judg. 2:10). This is why we need fathers and sons in ministry: to pass the inheritance from one generation to another.

Each generation is supposed to glean from both the successes and failures of the men and women of God who preceded them. We are called to worship the God of our fathers. Our experience should be just one glorious layer of spiritual riches upon another that have been increased as it passed from father to son.

God always meant there to be a magnification of revelation through the spiritual inheritance of the fathers being passed to the sons: "And the Lord thy God will bring thee into the land which thy fathers possessed, and thou shalt possess it; and He will do thee good, and multiply thee above thy fathers" (Deut 30:5). We can be multiplied above our fathers. Each generation should have a deeper relationship with God than their fathers did. It is the lack of generational understanding and concern that makes us unable to receive the impartation from previous generations. This causes the decrease of magnification and the loss of inheritance in the children of God.

We have dammed up the flow of generational blessings by not understanding our need for generational relationship. Our myopic mis-focus upon a "rapture" has caused us to see little need in passing our impartational inheritance to the next generation. Failing to provide for a future that we think will never arrive, we have lost our children and grandchildren to the world in mass numbers. Those children who do serve the

Lord have been forced to seek after God without the benefit of a father's blessing. We have forced each new age of understanding to go through a genesis of its own, instead of increasing it with the deposit of previous generations.

"And, ye fathers, provoke not your children to wrath: but bring them up in the nurture and admonition of the Lord" (Eph. 6:4). We have provoked our children to wrath because we removed the hope of future generations from their hearts! Why should they honor their fathers and mothers? Why should the present generation seek to learn from the past so they can be a blessing to their future? They see no future. We have so hammered the instantaneous "any second now" rapture mentality into their spirits that we have extinguished any passion for a generational pursuit in God.

I wholeheartedly believe in a literal, physical return of Christ upon the earth. I eagerly desire to see Him come in the clouds of glory. The problem is our intense focus on the final return of Christ. It has distracted us from the many comings and goings of Christ in our everyday life, the very manifestation of His presence that we desire. By so narrowing our focus, we have placed an indefinite hold on spiritual progression throughout our generations.

The flow of spiritual progression and digression flows from generation to generation. The following is a list of some things that are carried by this flow:

Iniquity (Ex. 20:5; 34:7; Deut. 5:9)
Righteousness (Deut. 7:9)
Illegitimacy (Deut. 23:2)

Impure heritage (Deut 23:3)
Revelation of the Lord (Deut. 29:29)
Fellowship with the Lord (Ex. 29:42)
Prayer (As "incense": Ps. 141:2; Ex. 30:8)
Atonement (Ex. 30:10). Rest (Ex. 31:16)
Anointing (Ex. 30:31; 40:15)
Offerings (Lev. 6:18; Num. 15:21)
Requirements for service (Lev. 10:9)
Disqualification for service (Lev. 21:17; 22:3)
Financial freedom (Lev. 25:30)
Garments (Ex. 28:4243; Num. 15:38)
Service (Num. 18:23)

All these and more flow from generation to generation, but our failure to acknowledge or participate in this order of God has disconnected true spiritual impartation in ministry.

How much have we lost because we failed to honor our fathers? What spiritual treasure could now reside in our lives, if we had only been in proper position to receive it? What unnecessary barrenness will be experienced by the next generation of ministry if order and flow are not reestablished in the present?

The first generation of the Church was awesome and mighty. The shadows of the apostles healed the sick and offering-thieves dropped dead in the middle of meetings. Buildings literally shook with the power of God as believers prayed and God answered. Lame men leaped and dead women were raised to life. Deacons held city-wide crusades, healed the sick, and cast out unclean spirits. The unchurched Gentiles spoke in tongues before a sermon was ever finished. Cities rioted, demons fled, and prison gates flew open. Prophetic voices predicted famines, future arrests, and storms at sea. Apostles spoke and sorcerers fumbled in blindness. Apostles preached and thousands upon thousands repented and were baptized in a single day. The world was turned upside-down in a single generation.

This first generation of the Church, who passed on the inheritance of the saints to the next generation of believers, gave us the blessings we enjoy today. The present loss of power and the current dilution of apostolic anointing is due to the destruction and negligence of generational connection.

Jesus expects the generations following Him to not only follow in His works, but even increase through the multiplication of spiritual inheritance through the generations. "Verily, verily, I say unto you, He that believeth on Me, the works that I do shall he do also; and greater works than these shall he do; because I go unto My Father" (Jn. 14:12). Isaiah prophesied, "Of the increase of His government and peace there shall be no end...from henceforth even for ever..." (Is. 9:7).

The first few generations of believers literally changed the world. The problem is, somewhere between then and now, the flow of generational blessing was disconnected. For centuries, every new generation in the Church has been forced into a new genesis of beginnings instead of rising higher in the flood of generational increase.

The only way we ever receive an inheritance in God is through the connection of the father and son. We needed redemption because, as sons of Adam, we inherited his sinful inclination. The necessity of being born again in order to enter into the Kingdom is based upon the spiritual fact that only members of a family receive an inheritance. By our spiritual connection with the Son of God, we become "children, then heirs; heirs of God, and joint-heirs with Christ" (Rom. 8:17a). Everything that comes from God to a believer comes in the form of an inheritance.

Our inheritance in God is to be treated with honor and respect. We are never to sell it at a price, as Esau did, who "despised his birthright" (see Gen. 25:29-34).

Esau's birthright was his right to a double portion of his father's house. Although many people feel that Jacob was deceitful, it is not a tale of treachery. Rather, it is the story of a sharp negotiator and a carnal customer. Esau was not tricked out of his birthright; he sold it. Esau sold not only his natural, but also his spiritual inheritance because he wanted to feed his flesh.

God hates the attitude of anyone who despises his birthright. This is why God says, "I loved Jacob, and I hated Esau" (see Mal. 1:2-3). Esau sold out his position of promise for a bowl of pottage.

Esau becomes a terrible type of a New Testament believer who cares more about his stomach than his soul, and more about material things than spiritual things. "Lest there be any fornicator, or profane person, as Esau, who for one morsel of meat sold his birthright. For ye know how that afterward, when he would have inherited the blessing, he was rejected: for he found no place of repentance, though he sought it carefully with tears" (Heb. 12:16-17).

There was no place of repentance in Esau's heart. There was no "turning toward the father." In this single act, Esau gave away all his tomorrows for one today. Esau closed the doors on his position of promise, severing the flow of blessing from father to son. He could have been in the ancestry of the Messiah, but Esau sold out and now will never birth a Christ into the world. The Messiah would be the seed of Jacob.

Selling the inheritance of his father was the issue between Naboth and Ahab:

> ***And Ahab spake unto Naboth, saying, Give me thy vine-yard, that I may have it for a garden of herbs, because it is near unto my house: and I will give thee for it a better vineyard than it; or, if it seem good to thee, I will give thee the worth of it in money. And Naboth said to Ahab, The Lord forbid it me, that I should give the inheritance of my fathers unto thee"* (1 Kings 21:2-3).**

Naboth refused to sell his vineyard for any price, even to serve the political machine of King Ahab. He could have gotten better lands, or perhaps lived in financial security for the rest of his days, but this was no ordinary piece of real estate. This was the inheritance of his father. This was his spiritual connection to the blessings of Abraham. God forbid that he sell out his inheritance in God for any price or any reason.

Naboth could not be bought, so he was killed. Jezebel had him murdered so her husband could enjoy a new piece of property. Of all the despicable acts of Ahab, this one received special recognition from God. The wrath of God was kindled when Ahab crossed the line of generational blessing and stole Naboth's inheritance in the Lord.

Elijah is sent to tell Ahab, "In the place where dogs licked the blood of Naboth shall dogs lick thy blood, even thine." (1 Kings 21:19). Elijah prophesied of the coming and of the location of Ahab's death; it would be at the place of his offense against God's inheritance. Yet the judgment of God was completed only by the death of all the seed of Ahab's house. The judgment for destroying an inheritance is that your inheritance is destroyed. Spiritual judgment is always released against those who violate spiritual inheritance (see Deut. 19:14; 27:17; Hos. 5:10).

Many in ministry today see no problem with removing boundaries and tampering with spiritual inheritance. The world of ministry is full of spiritual poachers like the pastor in the story at the beginning of this chapter. These are men who trespass proper boundaries and feed their congregations with sermons of stolen inspiration and meals of misbegotten messages obtained through another man's labor, which they claim to be their own.

This violates spiritual inheritance! Yet most feel as if nothing is wrong. The Bible says, "Therefore, behold, I am against the prophets, saith the Lord, that steal My words everyone from his neighbor" (Jer. 23:30). A son may use anything in his father's house, but when a "neighbor" takes something without permission, it is called theft

A spiritual father will spend years of prayer and decades of digging to hollow out a wellspring in his life. This is where the sweet waters of revelation gush forth into well-channeled brooks of spiritual relationship. Any true son is welcome to dip into these streams at any time. It is their right by inheritance.

Without relationship or right, however, pastoral pilfers and righteous robbers will sneak in the night and siphon stolen waters into the cisterns of their own spirits. That way no one will ever know that they do not have a source of living water within them.

No one has a copyright on Scripture, but revelation that was birthed through the travail of prayer and labor of seeking should not be taken by another and claimed as his own. The notes of a piano belong to every pianist, but the composition of notes into a melody belongs to its composer. Stealing it would be a crime. In ministry, stealing the composition of a melody of scriptural truth is a sin. It should not be taken and used outside the boundaries of relationship and inheritance.

The story of Elijah and Elisha strongly depicts the spiritual inheritance of father and son in the ministry. Running from Jezebel, Elijah is despondent and laments, "I am not better than my fathers" (1 Kings 19:4). The Lord answers Elijah's dilemma by instructing him to anoint Elisha as a "prophet in thy room" (1 Kings 19:16). Elisha served the man of God for several years, "pouring water on his hands" and following his ministry (see 2 Kings 3:11). Both of them knew that separation by fire was soon approaching:

> ***And it came to pass, when they were gone over, that Elijah said unto Elisha, Ask what I shall do for thee, before I be taken away from thee. And Elisha said, I pray thee, let a double portion of thy spirit be upon me. And he said, Thou hast asked a hard thing: nevertheless, if thou see me when I am taken from thee, it shall be so unto thee; but if not,***

***it shall not be so* (2 Kings 2:9-10).**

What Elisha requested was the spiritual inheritance of a firstborn son. Among the sons of a father, the oldest brother, the firstborn, would receive a double portion. "But he shall acknowledge the son of the hated for the firstborn, by giving him a double portion of all that he hath: for he is the beginning of his strength; the right of the firstborn is his" (Deut. 21:17). This means that the inheritance was divided by the number of brothers in the family. Then, according to the measure of each portion, the firstborn would receive double of what every other brother received. The firstborn became the leader of the family and received double honor (see 2 Chron. 21:3).

Other men besides Elisha also were called "sons of the prophets." Elisha does not slight them their due, but he is hungry for all of God that he can receive. He has followed Elijah in faithful service, never leaving his sight, knowing that he must be in proper position to receive a double portion.

Elisha knows that the only way he will become a father in the house is to be the firstborn son. The mark of the firstborn son is to "see the father when he goes." The term in Second Kings 2:10 is literally translated, "If you see me eye to eye." There must be a sharing of a common vision, an endurance of relationship and faithfulness to God and to each other in both father and son for inheritance to be transmitted. Esaus are not welcome here. Ten thousand tears do not qualify such a son in God's sight. It is only the turning of the heart that allows for proper alignment with the vision of a father.

With cascading mantles and cries of "My father, my father" the connection between spiritual generations is complete.

The Father's Inheritance

Elisha performs his ministry in double-portion power. The Church of today must recover generational connection and spiritual inheritance. The Church must return to God's order in ministry: the order of father to son.

Behold, I will send you Elijah the prophet before the coming of the great and dreadful day of the Lord: And he shall turn the heart of the fathers to the children, and the heart of the children to their fathers, lest I come and smite the earth with a curse.

                              Malachi 4:5-6

Chapter 4

The Father's Heart

The morning fog lay like a cotton quilt on the Tennessee hills surrounding the farm. Standing in a carport, I breathed deeply and thought, "No wonder they calls these the foothills of the Smokeys." A wisping vapor lifted gently from the spring and one of the rainbow trout (my pets) rose toward a frightened dragonfly above the surface of the pond. Walking around the little white Chevy pickup, I checked the bungee cords securing the bright blue tarp. Beneath the cover were all the earthly belongings of my youngest son.

Today he would begin that long drive to Texas. He was leaving for college. I silently thanked God that he had obediently submitted, grudgingly working through his first two years in junior college, fulfilling my request that he grow a little more. Now I would keep my word. He could go this third year anywhere he chose. More than a thousand thoughts sought my mental attention: Was he really ready? Had I prepared him sufficiently for the real and sinister world that awaited his arrival? Did he remember the conversations, the warnings, the life principles we had discussed and re-discussed in our recent days together? Had he casually listened or were those approving nods, signs of lasting mental photography, etching out portraits of reason and truth upon his fertile mind?

The new tires looked good. They should last out the next two years. Living on campus, he would not be driving that much: "He'll be home for Thanksgiving or at least Christmas," I hoped.

My mind turned to his decision to pursue a major in business management. Every preacher dad has a secret wish that one of his sons enters the ministry, but I had been consoled by his farsightedness concerning Kingdom things.

"Dad, don't you think we've been wrong in thinking that ministry has been equated mostly to preaching? It seems to me that if we are really Kingdom people, then everything we do in life should be considered our ministry. I want to bring a real Jesus into the business world. He has a right to be there too. Don't you think!" To this I had answered yes and canceled my preacher's speech.

The laundry room door opened and everything I was concerned about stood beside me dressed in jeans, sneakers, and a T-shirt boldly advertising Texas A&M. Before I could speak, he was on my neck and in my arms — my baby, my son, my man. "Dad, I'll remember. I love you, Daddy. Please don't worry." I watched the gravel lane grow empty and wept out loud, the morning sun faceting rainbows in my tears. The word of the apostle John embraced my frantic emotions. "I have no greater joy than to hear that my children walk in truth." (3 Jn. 4)

Moving slowly back toward the house, I remembered one of my mountain neighbors proudly saying that his son had graduated from Purdue University. Between chews and spits, this simple man stated that his son was now a successful businessman in Atlanta. "Makes us real proud, you know, and he never forgets Mom and me."

Here is the heart of a father - His son should do better, know more, go farther. Often our personal desires and possessive love would cause them to stay where we are or have them fulfill our own dreams. Selfishly we would make them servants to our personal agendas. Yet every true Dad knows that the day will come when his own dreams will drive away.

> **B**ehold, I will send you Elijah the prophet before the coming of the great and dreadful day of the Lord: and he shall turn the heart of the fathers to the children, and the heart of the children to their fathers, lest I come and smite the earth with a curse (Malachi 4:5-6).

These two verses of Scripture are the final verses of the entire Old Testament. These words are the focal point of an entire era of revelation. The height and apex of all 40 books in over half our Bible are suddenly stopped at these verses. Two thousand years of God's relationship with man end in these sentences. The entire age of kings and prophets culminate in these words.

These two verses contain a prophecy, a promise of blessing and the threat of a curse all at the same time. The prophecy is that Elijah will come before the day of the Lord. The promise of blessing is that the relationship between "fathers" and "sons" will be restored. The curse is that if there is not a "turning of hearts," the earth will be smitten with a curse.

This prophecy has always been taken very seriously by the Jewish people. The Passover feast is still kept by millions of the descendants of the Exodus. This feast time is used to remember past blessings, as well as to look forward to future events in God's timetable. Every year at their Passover celebration, the table settings include one for the coming of Elijah. An extra plate and glass of wine are set aside; no one is allowed to use it. Abraham's children are taught to expect Elijah to come.

Does the Church have a place ready for Elijah? As Christians, who are followers of the complete revelation of God, do we have a setting in the life of the Body for an Elijah to return and be welcomed?

Both times when Elijah or the spirit of Elijah did come before, the leaders of God's people found no place for him. Will the Church receive him now? Are we any better than our fathers?

The mention of "both times" is not an error in printing. Elijah came the first time in the days of Ahab, and the spirit of Elijah came the second time in the person of John the Baptist.

The final prophecy of the Old Testament sailed like a spear cast from the hand of God through 400 years of silence to land its point at the feet of Zacharias. As he offered incense upon the altar, an angel came to the father of John with a message about the child that would come to his house: "And he shall go before him in the spirit and power of Elias, to turn the hearts of the fathers to the children, and the disobedient to the wisdom of the just; to make ready a people prepared for the Lord." (Lk. 1:17). When Zacharias did not receive the word of the Lord, he was struck silent like the 400 years before him. Similarly, the Church will not have a true voice until fathers receive the word of the Lord and turn toward their sons. Then, like Zacharias, they will speak "full of the Holy Spirit" (see Lk. 1:67).

The sending of Elijah is a preparation for the return of Christ upon the earth. God could have sent another Moses to deliver His people. He could have sent a Jeremiah or Isaiah if He needed a prophet He could have sent Enoch if He wanted someone whom He took from the earth without seeing death. He could have sent a Joseph or Solomon if He wanted wisdom on the earth again. Or God could have sent a David if He wanted praise and worship to prepare for His coming.

The key question is this: Why does God send the "spirit and power of Elijah" to prepare for His arrival? Why not somebody else? Why must Elijah, or someone in "the power and spirit of Elijah/' come back before the Lord does?

Elijah is the only person in the Bible who passed a double portion of his spirit to a son in the ministry. Considering our study in previous chapters, the term *fathers* refers to fathers in the ministry of the Kingdom of God. The term children refers to those sons and daughters who follow a ministry father. This is why the Lord "will send you Elijah the prophet before the coming of the great and dreadful day of the Lord." The Lord wants His Church to minister in the power of double portions. God wants His people to pass their inheritance in ministry to the next generation so the increase and expansion of the Kingdom will grow from father to son. Consider the increase of miracles between Elijah and Elisha.

Elijah experienced at least 14 miraculous acts in his ministry:

Three years of drought (1 Kings 17:1)
Being fed by ravens (1 Kings 17:2-7)

Multiplying of meal and oil (1 Kings 17:8-16)
Resurrection of young child (1 Kings 17:17-24)
Calling down fire from Heaven (1 Kings 18:30-40)
Prayer for rain answered (1 Kings 18:41-45)
Outrunning a chariot for miles (1 Kings 18:46)
Living 40 days and nights on divine sustenance (1 Kings 19:8)
Prophecy of the death of Ahab and Jezebel (1 Kings 21:17-24)
Prophecy of Jehoram's death (2 Chron. 21:12-15)
Prophecy of Ahaziah's death (2 Kings 1:2-8)
Calling down fire from Heaven again (2 Kings 1:10-12)
Parting of the waters of Jordan (2 Kings 2:7-8)
Departing by a whirlwind into Heaven (2 Kings 2:11)

Elisha experienced at least 28 miraculous events in his ministry:
Parting of the waters of Jordan (2 Kings 2:13-15)
Healing of waters (2 Kings 2:19-22)
Bears mauling disrespectful youths (2 Kings 2:23-25)
Water filling ditches (2 Kings 3:16-20)
Prophecy of the defeat of the Moabites (2 Kings 3:18-20;24-27)
Increase of widow's oil (2 Kings 4:1-7)
Barren woman gives birth (2 Kings 4:12-17)
Resurrection of child (2 Kings 4:32-37)
Pottage made healthy (2 Kings 4:38-41)
Bread multiplied (2 Kings 4:42-44)
Leprosy healed (2 Kings 5:1-14)
Discernment of Gehazi's actions (2 Kings 5:25-26)
Leprosy of Gehazi (2 Kings 5:27)

Making axehead float (2 Kings 6:1-7)
Revealing war secrets (2 Kings 6:8-12)
Servant seeing heavenly host (2 Kings 6:13-17)
Blinding Syrian army (2 Kings 6:18)
Healing Syrian army of blindness (2 Kings 6:20-23)
Knowledge of king's act (2 Kings 6:32-33)
Prophecy of famine end (2 Kings 7:1)
Prophecy of soldier's death (2 Kings 7:2)
Confusion of Syrians (2 Kings 7:6-8)
Seven years of famine (2 Kings 8:1-2)
Prophecy of recovery and death (2 Kings 8:7-11)
Prophecy of murder and kingship (2 Kings 8:12-13)
Anointing and prophecy of Jehu (2 Kings 9:1-10)
Prophecy of victory (2 Kings 13:14-19)
Resurrection of man (2 Kings 13:21)

Elisha experienced twice as many miracles as Elijah. God desires for His Kingdom to be manifested in the life of His people in the fullness of double-portion ministry. Yet this can only happen if, like Elijah, fathers in the ministry turn their hearts toward their sons. The father's heart must turn toward sons first; then sons can turn to fathers. If not, God will smite the earth with a curse.

First, though, ministry must develop the heart of a father. When we observe the lives of ministry fathers in the Bible, we see how the heart of a father in ministry is defined and developed.

The heart of a father is formed by the wilderness experiences of life and ministry. Elijah lived alone in the wilderness. John the Baptist, who came in the spirit and power of Elijah, followed the same pattern of being alone with God.

"And the child grew, and waxed strong in spirit, and was in the deserts till the day of his shewing unto Israel." (Lk. 1:80).

Notice how the words of the following verses are placed side by side: "Annas and Caiaphas being the high priests, the word of God came unto John the son of Zacharias in the wilderness." (Lk. 3:2). The religious establishment was in a corrupt, perverse situation. There are two high priests when there should only be one! Neither of these men knew God. These men served in the temple every day, yet the word of the Lord does not come to them. The word comes to John in the wilderness.

Moses was in the desert before showing up in Pharaoh's court with the word of the Lord in his mouth. The exodus of God's people out of Egypt came only because a father in the ministry walked out of the wilderness.

Often the wilderness is a time of transition. It takes you out of the comfort of mediocrity. It takes away everything that you thought you had to have and turns your heart toward what you really need. It becomes the sterile environment God needs to perform a heart transplant.

Do not curse your wilderness and do not expect the Christian community to wholly embrace your spiritual alteration. This heart operation cannot be accomplished in sterile religious clinics or on the comfortable theological couches of the modern Church. True fathers and sons will have walked and wandered the forsaken lonely wilderness paths of purpose, pace, and process.

Being lost in the wilderness is the only way fathers find

themselves. Through the pain and cost of following the Lord through the difficult circumstances of their unique callings, they blaze a trail for others to follow. Should sons be expected to cross the raging rivers of their present experience without a bridge built by a father laying down his life? Where is the example in our lives of submission, commitment, and honor? Should fathers expect absolute order from those who follow them when their own lives are filled with failed principles and out-of-order precepts? Are we asking for what we refuse to give?

God prepares a father's heart by calling him to receive from a family that has no father. When the brook Cherith dried up, God sent Elijah to such a family: "Arise, get thee to Zarephath, which belongeth to Zidon, and dwell there: behold, I have commanded a widow woman there to sustain thee." (1 Kings 17:9). The fatherless were powerless in the days of the Bible. Part of a father's heart must be toward those who are fatherless in ministry.

Elijah causes a great miracle of supply in the house of the widow and her son. He will also, by intercession, bring her dead son back to life.

> *And he cried unto the Lord, and said, O Lord my God, hast Thou also brought evil upon the widow with whom I sojourn, by slaying her son? And he stretched himself upon the child three times, and cried unto the Lord, and said, O Lord my God, I pray Thee, let this child's soul come into him again. And the Lord heard the voice of Elijah; and the soul of the child came into him again, and he revived. And Elijah took the child, and brought him down out of the chamber into the house, and delivered him unto his mother: and Elijah said,*

See, thy son liveth. And the woman said to Elijah, Now by this I know that thou art a man of God, and that the word of the Lord in thy mouth is truth. **(1 Kings 17:20-24).**

Elijah first appeared to this woman at the city gate, and her obedience to feed him caused a miraculous supply to come to her house. It was a great miracle, but she still was not sure of this God he served, or this man of God... until Elijah raised her son from the dead. Then she said "Now by this I know that thou art a man of God, and that the word of the Lord in thy mouth is truth." This widow woman did not think Elijah was a man of God until, through the love and concern of a father's heart, he prayed for her son and God raised him from the dead. With her last meal and a miracle she served Elijah. With the return of her boy, Elijah's ministry served her. The heart of a father prays for sons to live. God's heart is revealed through the unselfish intercession of Elijah. The widow now knew that God cared for her. The father's heart was shown and her heart was won to the Father.

Elijah then cast his mantle upon a farm boy named Elisha. Elisha received it first as a call to service. Later he wore it as a double-portion increase of inheritance. All that Elisha would ever be in ministry was based on the heart of his father in ministry, who obeyed the Lord and anointed a "prophet in thy room." (1 Kings 19:16).

John the Baptist was the bridge over which the blessings and promises of the fathers in the Old Testament were carried to the children of the Kingdom of God initiated in the ministry of Jesus. John prepared a way for all the generations that followed him to know God in a relationship that all the generations before him could only know in their dreams.

This is why Jesus could say of John:

Verily I say unto you, Among them that are born of women there hath not risen a greater than John the Baptist: notwithstanding he that is least in the kingdom of heaven is greater than he. And from the days of John the Baptist until now the kingdom of heaven suffereth violence, and the violent take it by force. For all the prophets and the law prophesied until John. And if ye will receive it, this is Elias, which was for to come. He that hath ears to hear, let him hear **(Matthew 11:11-15)**.

John was the greatest of men, but the least in the Kingdom. John had the heart of a father. A father wants the next generation to be greater than he could ever imagine.

The disciples of John the Baptist were concerned that his ministry was being eclipsed by the One he baptized.

And they came unto John, and said unto him, Rabbi, he that was with thee beyond Jordan, to whom thou barest witness, behold, the same baptizeth, and all men come to Him. John answered...this my joy therefore is fulfilled. He must increase, but I must decrease **(John 3:26-30)**.

This is the turning of fathers' hearts toward the children. This is the spirit of Elijah that must be sent from God before the great and dreadful day of the Lord. Ministry must not rest until it has blessed the next generation with the mantle of its anointing. Fathers can no longer serve only their own ministry; they must desire their son in the ministry to exceed all limits of their own time. The fathers must decrease and the sons must increase...or God will smite the earth with a curse.

The greatest ministry of Elijah was not his miracles, but his son. Elisha healed lepers, separated water from dry land, and multiplied a few loaves of bread to feed a hundred men. He was so full of power that entire armies could not defeat him. Yet he would have lived and died behind a plow if Elijah had not given everything he had to this firstborn of his ministry.

John the Baptist lived in a wilderness. He ate wild food and wore strange garments. He preached under the sun by the Jordan River. John did no miracle because he prepared the way for the greatest Miracle Worker of all time.

The apostle John describes the heart of a father: "I have no greater joy than to hear that my children walk in truth." (3 Jn. 4). The heart of the father desires his son to not only match the blessings in his own life, but also to exceed them. This is the heart of Elijah, and of all those who come in his spirit.

Any ministry that lives to itself and builds for itself will die by itself. The father in ministry is not threatened by the rise of the son's ministry above his own. Instead, he rejoices that he had a part in the development of something greater than he could ever have dreamed possible.

Generations of Jews have prepared a place at their Passover meal for Elijah to return. Centuries of empty plates waiting to be filled is a picture of the hunger for a ministry with a father's heart. Their desire was fulfilled by the coming of John the Baptist, who heralded their Messiah. Today God's desire is for His Church to live in the double portion of His Spirit. The heart of the fathers must turn toward the children. We must see the increase of God's power fill the earth!

He that is born in thy house, and he that is bought with thy money, must needs be circumcised: and My covenant shall be in your flesh for an everlasting covenant.

Genesis 17:13

Chapter 5

The Father's Covenant

He made you go to bed when you wanted to stay up and play.

He made you eat vegetables with names like artichoke and squash.

He made you wash the car once a week and take out the trash every day.

Homework always came first before television, and on Sunday mornings

He made you go to church when all your friends go to sleep in.

For a summer vacation, he took you to see your grandparents, aunts, uncles, and cousins ...

When you wanted to go to the beach in Florida.

You Have Not Many Fathers

His demands never seem to end! They stood like a guard between you and total freedom.

Where you stand today dressed in a blue cap and gown,

The tassel of your cap, like the hands of a clock,,

Changed sides to denote a new direction: out on your own into the world.

Suddenly home didn't seem so bad.

The chores, the curfews, and the rules seem light

As you now feel the full weight of adult responsibility

You now know why your father's shoulders stoop just a bit.

It is such a heavy burden, but one you can carry

You stand with straight posture because of a father who made you reach higher.

He gave you a framework of rest and hard work; heritage and faith

In a balance of discipline and love.

You are the product of a man's determination to see you succeed.

And for the last 18 years of his life that he gave to you,

He receives your success as payment in full.

It is ironic that it is here, at the crossroads of your life, where you finally meet your Dad.

It is the place where you come to see him eye to eye.

The Father's Covenant

Just as God has caused the earth to turn toward the sun,

He has caused the son to turn toward the father.

It is the rotation of warmth and light that continues from generation to generation

Until we meet at the cross

Of a father and son.

The revelation of God to His covenant people has always been in the order of father to son. That is how we embrace our status as the children of God and how we receive salvation and relationship with God. This is our inheritance as "heirs of God, and joint-heirs with Christ" (Rom. 8:17). Our relationship with God is a reflection of the order of father and son.

We must also understand that ministry relationships are to reflect the order of father and son as well. However, because the Church has not realized the essence of father-and-son relationship in ministry, we do not receive our inheritance. Our adaptation of other models has caused the Church to lose connection with spiritual inheritance.

Although God has given us all things in Christ, the Church has not received the fullness of that inheritance because her ministry is not manifested in father-and-son relationships. This is why God is sending us the spirit of Elijah. God will restore the alignment between fathers and sons in the ministry.

The relationship between father and son in the ministry is more than an employee/boss relationship. It is more than the business arrangement of president and vice-president, or manager and assistant manager. The Church is an outpost of the Kingdom of God - a God who always deals in relational terms. God's actions and expression are the revelation of His person and essence, and God revealed Himself to us in terms of relationship: Father, Son, and Spirit.

The Father's Covenant

He created and redeemed us, and we are His children. God requires that the covenant He made with us through His Son also be the model for all relationships in the Kingdom. The word *covenant* means "to cut." The sign of a covenant relationship between God and the seed of Abraham is the cut of circumcision.

After centuries of bitter bondage, God raised up Moses and set him as the man to lead the people of God into the freedom of divine purpose. Moses was drawn out of a woven womb in the Nile to become "learned in all the wisdom of the Egyptians" (Acts 7:22). Upon realization of his place in the plan of God, "esteeming the reproach of Christ greater riches than the treasures in Egypt" (Heb. 11:26a), Moses lived for 40 years in the Midian wilderness and "begat" two sons. The angel of the Lord appeared to Moses in a burning bush, revealed His name, and gave this stuttering shepherd the power to cripple the pride of Pharaoh. With all that Moses was and was to become, when Moses obeyed his call and went toward Egypt, God came to Moses to kill him:

> ***And it came to pass by the way in the inn, that the Lord met him, and sought to kill him. Then Zipporah took a sharp stone, and cut off the foreskin of her son, and cast it at his feet, and said, Surely a bloody husband art thou to me. So He let him go: then she said, A bloody husband thou art, because of the circumcision.* (Exodus 4:24-26).**

This man Moses—giver of the Law, author of the Torah, prophet like unto Christ—did not fulfill his duty as a father to his sons and circumcise them. God will invest 80 years in a man, developing him to be the deliverer of His people. He will patiently endure the halting stride of a baby Moses, and his maturation process of falling and stumbling as he learned to walk before God. However, if the man of God does not align his life with the order of God, God will come to kill him. God will not allow His order to be cast aside, even to fulfill His will in the earth.

The question is this: Does God love us any more than He loved Moses? What makes us think that we can run the Church any way we please and God will spare us from His wrath?

We must turn our hearts. We must return to the order of father and son in ministry. God would not have spared Moses if he did not properly father the nation that he was to lead to deliverance. We must have fathers who will be a father to sons. We must have fathers who will circumcise their sons.

Some may fail to see the significance of the rite of circumcision for today. Any student of the New Testament and of the writings of Paul will tell you that the rite of circumcision is totally unnecessary for salvation. Of course, that is correct. The apostle Paul vehemently opposed any attempt by the religious-bent teachers of his day to make any requirement for salvation outside of faith in Christ.

The apostle Paul writes against circumcision throughout his epistles (see Rom. 2:25-29; 1 Cor. 7:18-19; Gal. 5:11-12; Phil. 3:2-3; Col. 2:10-11; Tit. 1:10-11). Paul is so opposed to those who teach circumcision that he calls them "dogs" and the "concision," which means "mutilators of the flesh." Paul would just as well they were "cut off," literally meaning they should just castrate themselves (see Gal. 5:12). This is extremely strong language, even for the apostle Paul. To say that Paul is resolutely against the rite of circumcision is a huge understatement.

That is why the following account of Paul in the Book of Acts is so strange:

> ***Then came he to Derbe and Lystra: and, behold, a certain disciple was there, named Timotheus, the son of a certain woman, which was a Jewess, and believed; but his father was a Greek: which was well reported of by the brethren that were at Lystra and Iconium. Him would Paul have to go forth with him; and took and circumcised him because of the Jews which were in those quarters: for they knew all that his father was a Greek*** (Acts 16:1-3).

At first glance, one might think that Paul was hypocritical. The apostle said so much against circumcision in so many letters. Yet here we see him circumcising an adult believer. His words and his actions seem to conflict, until you understand that Timothy's circumcision was not a matter of salvation. Timothy was already a believer. His circumcision was not for salvation; it was the act of a father in ministry to a son in the gospel.

Paul was traveling through the twin cities of Derbe and Lystra when he found a young man who would become his "dearly beloved son" (2 Tim 1:2). Timothy was extremely well-versed in Scripture and raised in a multi-generational foundation in Christ. Both his mother and grandmother were mentioned by name as training Timothy in godliness. "When I call to remembrance the unfeigned faith that is in thee, which dwelt first in thy grandmother Lois, and thy mother Eunice; and I am persuaded that in thee also" (2 Tim. 1:5). "And that from a child thou hast known the holy scriptures, which are able to make thee wise unto salvation through faith which is in Christ Jesus." (2 Tim. 3:15).

Timothy is referred to as a disciple, a true believer in Jesus. He was highly recommended by the brethren of other fellowships as well as by his own. Timothy had evidently been involved in the ministry in a local and even trans-local level. Obviously, Timothy was eminently qualified as a candidate for ministry with Paul. There was only one problem. One thing is mentioned twice in the first three verses of Acts 16: "his father was a Greek."

Timothy was already a believer when he met Paul. Evidently, Timothy was raised as a believer or became a disciple rather early in his life. Thus Paul did not circumcise Timothy for salvation. Paul circumcised him for ministry. Timothy's father was a Greek; he is not mentioned as a believer. Even if he was a believer, Timothy had not been properly fathered by anyone for ministry. Paul did not circumcise him so he would be accepted by God, but accepted by men. It was an act of a father to a son in preparation for ministry.

This does not mean that ministry people must meet some sort of physical requirement as a qualification for service. Circumcision was always more than a physical mark. It was a sign of the covenant of the generations of Abraham. It was a token of their obedience to God. It was a sign that each son of Abraham would pass on to his son as a mark of generational inheritance in God. It was a sign of the circumcision of the heart.

Circumcision of the heart implies total devotion to God.

> *Only the Lord had a delight in thy fathers to love them, and He chose their seed after them, even you above all people, as it is this day. Circumcise therefore the foreskin of your heart, and be no more stiffnecked* **(Deuteronomy 10:15-16).**

> *Circumcise yourselves to the Lord, and take away the foreskins of your heart, ye men of Judah and inhabitants of Jerusalem: lest My fury come forth like fire, and burn that none can quench it, because of the evil of your doings* **(Jeremiah 4:4).**

When circumcision of the heart is mentioned in the Bible, we know that it does not mean open-heart surgery. It is not literal surgery, but spiritual surgery that God performs on His people. Circumcision has always been an external sign of an internal singularity of devotion to Yahweh. The cutting away of flesh is symbolic of cutting away anything "fleshy" in the heart relationship between God and His people. God has never considered the removal of a physical foreskin without true relationship to be a sign of salvation.

Thus circumcision was more than a sign of the covenant. It was a necessary spiritual surgical procedure that had to take place for ministry to be in proper order. If there is no circumcision of the heart, then the ability to hear the voice of God is muffled, as if the ears are covered with flesh. The prophet Jeremiah said as much: "To whom shall I speak, and give warning, that they may hear? Behold, their ear is uncircumcised, and they cannot hearken: behold, the word of the Lord is unto them a reproach; they have no delight in it." (Jer. 6:10). The first martyr of the church, deacon Stephen, felt the same way about the heart problem affecting the ability to hear the word of the Lord: "Ye stiffnecked and uncircumcised in heart and ears, ye do always resist the Holy Ghost as your fathers did, so do ye" (Acts 7:51). It is the uncircumcised heart of the "circumcised" religious leaders that deafened their ears to the voice of the Spirit.

When Paul circumcised Timothy, it was more than just a physical, outward sign. Circumcision has always made a spiritual scar—a permanent mark for an everlasting covenant. It was a spiritual operation to cut away the flesh from the heart of a son in the ministry. It is something that must be done by a father in the ministry, so the son can proceed with hearing ears and an open heart

A son in the ministry must place his life into the hands of a spiritual father. If Timothy was to minister the gospel to his full effectiveness, he had to yield his life to Paul. This vulnerability is an openness to change and impartation. It is a quality of trust that a child has for his father. It is the close relationship of family where problems, mistakes, and imperfections, as well as hopes, dreams, and desires, are made known in the security of commitment. The son must fully trust his father to perform the painful surgery in proper righteousness. He must become an Isaac, allowing his father to bind him with cords, and yield to a sharpened knife.

Before Moses could deliver the people, he had to circumcise his son. Although a father in the ministry will be the instrument, God is the source of the circumcision. "And the Lord thy God will circumcise thine heart, and the heart of thy seed, to love the Lord thy God with all thine heart, and with all thy soul, that thou mayest live" (Deut. 30:6). God cuts on every man in His house. He will allow no one to escape the removal of flesh.

A son in the ministry must understand that what may feel like an offense in the flesh is actually the removal of offense in his life. Some will flinch at the first feeling of pain and run away. Bleeding, they feel wounded instead of honored to be a son. They become offended by the attempt to remove their flesh. Some will abandon a father's house and accuse him of abuse that never occurred. Led by the pain of their wounding instead of by the Spirit, they prove by their slanderous departure their need for circumcision. The part that is bleeding and in need of attention is the very part that needed removal. Sadly the son will go from one father's house to another, hopping from church to church, leaving a trail of blood behind him. The son will cry of his "wounding" until he can find someone who will listen and refuse to cut on him as a son. The son, in seeking to escape pain, escapes from purpose and identity in God. In refusing to have his flesh cut off, he is "cut off" from his potential in the Kingdom.

The proper response is to follow the example of the Joshua generation: "And it came to pass, when they had done circumcising all the people, that they abode in their places in the camp, till they were whole" (Josh. 5:8). When a son is cut by a father in the ministry, he should stay where he is until the wounding is healed, before he continues further in ministry. Otherwise, the source of direction in ministry may be the leading of pain instead of the purpose of the Spirit. Sons must be led by the Spirit, not the flesh. "For if ye live after the flesh, ye shall die: but if ye through the Spirit do mortify the deeds of the body, ye shall live. For as many as are led by the Spirit of God, they are the sons of God" (Rom. 8:13-14).

A father in the ministry circumcises the son by dealing with an area of the flesh that must be removed from the son's life. He cannot cut too much, or the father may destroy a son's ability to be a father. Yet the father must cut his son, or that son will never enter the fullness of his purpose. It is a delicate spiritual operation that must be carried out with the heart of a father. A father is willing to cause discomfort only so the son may excel even beyond the ministry of the father.

Some men called to be fathers resist entering into covenant relationship with a son in the ministry because of the pain inherently involved in such a commitment. A manager/employee or a team/coach model of relationship is preferred to the intimacy of a father to son by many in church leadership. Employees are paid to do something. Sons are brought up to become something. The order of father and son is so intrinsic to the very nature of the Kingdom of God that to allow any other type of relational model in the Church is to cease reflecting the very Kingdom of our proclamation.

Fathers who do not circumcise their sons leave them as bastards, not as sons. They in turn will not circumcise, and the generations of illegitimate ministry will continue. "A bastard shall not enter into the congregation of the Lord; even to his tenth generation shall he not enter into the congregation of the Lord" (Deut. 23:2). By not following the order of father and son, we have fathers with clean hands but impure hearts. They are not willing to raise up anyone but themselves as the head of the house. They will not cut into a son because they will not be responsible to care for his wound. They would rather rule over an employee than raise a son.

Any man can sire a child. Any man of normal health can have a sexual relationship with a woman and produce children. That is not being a father. That is simply producing a child. A father does more than just have children. He raises his children to become mature adults. It is a painful, costly, time-consuming, life-draining, "stay up at all hours of the night" type of relationship. It is not always a joyful experience for the father or the son. The cost is everything a father has within him. The benefit is a son who will honor his father.

The absence of a father's care in a son's life is the abuse of neglect. Failure to circumcise a son is the painful mark of a father who does not care. However, there is more than one type of abuse in the family of God.

There are abusive men in the Church who say they have the heart of a father, yet wield the knife of a butcher. Some will cut on a son with the heart of Simeon and Levi, not with the heart of a father.

> ***And the sons of Jacob answered Shechem and Hamor his father deceitfully, and said, because he had defiled Dinah their sister: and they said unto them, We cannot do this thing, to give our sister to one that is uncircumcised; for that were a reproach unto us: but in this will we consent unto you: If ye will be as we be, that every male of you be circumcised*** (Genesis 34:13-15).

Simeon and Levi were not true fathers, but rebellious sons who did not have the heart of their father, Jacob.

They killed all the men of Shechem, taking advantage of their wounding. They took the city captive and all the food, animals, women, and children were taken as spoil. The sign of covenant relationship was used as revenge.

There are some men in the Church who castrate all the sons beneath them in order to be the only source of production in the house. A man who is insecure in his ability in fatherhood becomes a destroyer of all who might be able to become a father. He makes all who labor with him be servants, not sons. Those sons are eunuchs, not potential fathers. That is not covenant relationship, but the management of hirelings. It is not the heart of a father. Such a man is an abusive father. He only wounds to take something away, not to give everything to the son. Sadly, many of these abusive fathers exist in the Church today.

God does not honor this type of abuse, and a true father in the ministry rejects it. Jacob said to Simeon and Levi "...Ye have troubled me to make me to stink among the inhabitants of the land...I shall be destroyed, I and my house" (Gen. 34:30). On his deathbed, Jacob does not give them a blessing, but a curse.

> ***Simeon and Levi are brethren; instruments of cruelty are in their habitations. O my soul, come not thou into their secret; unto their assembly, mine honor, be not thou united: for in their anger they slew a man, and in their selfwill they digged down a wall. Cursed be their anger, for it was fierce; and their wrath, for it was cruel: I will divide them in Jacob, and scatter them in Israel*** **(Genesis 49:5-7).**

False fathers castrate sons by cutting away any possibility for the sons to bear their own house. They are "instruments of cruelty...in their habitations." They do not walk in love, but anger and wrath. "And, ye fathers, provoke not your children to wrath: but bring them up in the nurture and admonition of the Lord" (Eph. 6:4).

And when Abram was ninety years old and nine, the Lord appeared to Abram, and said unto him, I am the Almighty God; walk before Me, and be thou perfect And I will make My covenant between Me and thee, and will multiply thee exceedingly. ... Neither shall thy name any more be called Abram, but thy name shall be Abraham; for a father of many nations have I made thee. ... And God said unto Abraham, Thou shalt keep My covenant therefore, thou, and thy seed after thee in their generations. This is My covenant, which ye shall keep, between Me and you and thy seed after thee; Every man child among you shall be circumcised. And ye shall circumcise the flesh of your foreskin; and it shall be a token of the covenant betwixt Me and you. And he that is eight days old shall be circumcised among you, every man child in your generations, he that is born in the house, or bought with money of any stranger, which is not of thy seed. He that is born in thy house, and he that is bought with thy money, must needs be circumcised: and My covenant shall be in your flesh for an everlasting covenant. And the uncircumcised man child whose flesh of his foreskin is not circumcised, that soul shall be cut off from his people; he hath broken My covenant **(Genesis 17:1-2,5,9-14).**

Abraham circumcised every male that was in his house, whether he was a bought slave or born in the house as a slave. Whether they were of the seed of Abraham or not, the act of the order of father to son had to be followed. Everyone who carried seed in the house of Abraham had to be circumcised. The father is the head of the house. He bears the responsibility that each person in his house follow the Lord and worship the Lord properly. This is why Abraham had to circumcise not only his natural children, but also all those in his house.

Each local church is the house of a father. The father of the ministry in the church is the one who is ultimately responsible for the congregation's proper training and worship of the Lord. Paul addressed the Corinthian congregation with the understanding that as their father in the ministry, he was the father of their house and the one most qualified to speak truth into their lives. "For though ye have ten thousand instructors in Christ, yet have ye not many fathers: for in Christ Jesus I have begotten you through the gospel" (1 Cor 4:15).

The ministry of a father in the local church is to train those under him to follow him as he follows Christ. He is the one who carries the flinty knife of fatherhood and circumcises sons for ministry. The father of a house must make sure that everyone born in the house has been circumcised. Every son in the family line must receive the same sign. Every son is to bear the same image as his father. The father also must make sure that every guest ministry or any paid staff member who comes into the house speaks from a circumcised heart as well"...every man child in your generations, he that is born in the house, or bought with money of any stranger, which is not of thy seed. He that is born in thy house, and he that is bought with thy money, must needs be circumcised..." (Gen. 17:12-13).

The Lord gave the order of circumcision to Abram at the same time He changed his name to Abraham. "Neither shall thy name any more be called Abram, but thy name shall be Abraham; for a father of many nations have I made thee" (Gen. 17:5). Abram means "high father" and Abraham means "father of a multitude." Abraham received a new name when he received the revelation concerning circumcision. Abraham's identity was established in his covenant relationship with God at the same time circumcision was established as the identification mark of the covenant. Thus circumcision was the time when the male child received his name and his identity.

Abraham was instructed to circumcise his seed on the eighth day of their birth (see Acts 7:8; Phil. 3:5). The eighth day is significant in the order of father and son because the same number of days was necessary for consecrating the sons of Aaron to their father's office. Although discussed again later in Chapter 8, the sons of Aaron were not anointed with oil. Only Aaron received the anointing as the head of the priesthood. His sons received the anointing by wearing their father's garments for seven days. On the eighth day, the period of their consecration ended (see Lev. 8:6-13; 8:30-9:1).

On the eighth day they emerged from the house of God with their father Aaron as sons in the ministry. It is on this day that the sons of Aaron receive their identity. Also, both Jesus and John the Baptist were given their names on the eighth day when they were circumcised.

> *And it came to pass, that on the eighth day they came to circumcise the child; and they called him Zacharias, after the name of his father. And his mother answered and said, Not so; but he shall be called John. And they said unto her, There is none of thy kindred that is called by this name. And they made signs to his father, how he would have him called. And he asked for a writing table, and wrote, saying, His name is John. And they mar-veiled all. And his mouth was opened immediately, and his tongue loosed, and he spake, and praised God* **(Luke 1:59-64).**

This giving of the name "John" was significant because it was not a name from the natural order of his father. The relatives present at the circumcision assumed that the child would be named after his father, Zacharias, until Elisabeth intervened. This son was not to follow the route of his natural father.

God is calling a generation of leaders to stop following old patterns of ministry that we have known in our past God is calling fathers to turn their hearts to sons, and sons to fathers. This needs to be the new basis for identity in ministry. It will seem strange to many. They will not understand, and say "There is none of thy kindred that is called by this name." This return of Kingdom relationship to ministry must resist every trend to be labeled and categorized.

Zacharias was the father of John in the physical sense, but not necessarily in the spiritual. John was not to follow in the priesthood of Aaron. John would not follow a system that had no voice. John would become "the voice of one crying in the wilderness, Prepare ye the way of the Lord, make His paths straight" (Lk. 3:4). Zacharias served in the temple; John would be found in the wilderness. John would not be named after his father. "John" would be the name of the man who would turn the hearts of the fathers to the sons. Though John was given his identity by his father at his circumcision, it was the spirit and power of Elijah that formed his ministry.

Joseph and Mary also named their son according to angelic instruction on the day of His circumcision. "And when eight days were accomplished for the circumcising of the child, His name was called JESUS, which was so named of the angel before He was conceived in the womb" (Lk. 2:21). The blood of Jesus is always associated with the power of His name. When we say "in the name of Jesus," we call on everything within His person and identity. The naming of a son was done at circumcision because it was that rite that granted covenant identity to physical identity.

If sons are properly fathered into their ministry, then they in turn will be able to father their own sons. The curse of an illegitimate ministry is turned into a blessing of immeasurable proportions. The father receives great honor from the sons who follow in his path. The sons increase with each generation as they pass layers of blessing upon blessing to the sons who follow them.

We live in a generation of Timothys. The Church is full of men who have been well-nursed in the bosom of the Church, but never fathered by the ministry of an apostle. Many leaders in the Church have enjoyed the process of spiritual conception; few have ever taken the responsibility of being a father. Today's Church is flooded with speaking ministries that produce momentary excitement that in turn propagates revelatory expulsions. What God desires is fathers who will "travail until Christ be formed" by the reality of covenant relationship.

And there came a voice from heaven, saying, Thou art My beloved Son, in whom I am well pleased.

Mark 1:11

Chapter 6

The Father's Voice

There was a man in the early days of my pastorate in Fort Worth named David. David was introduced to us by a nurse named Pat, who was a member of our congregation. She worked at a rest home where David was a resident. David used to work as an engineer who created, designed, and tested safety equipment within jet airplanes. One day David was testing an ejection set and had fully armed the device he was seated in to make sure it functioned properly. Actual operation was never intended in this test module. A reckless workman came by and released a lever that propelled David 40 feet in the steel rafters of the building. When they removed David from the infrastructure of the ceiling, he was breathing and alive, but his body was completely paralyzed.

David had been in the paralyzed condition for several years when Pat informed some men in our church that his doctors had asked for volunteers to assist in giving David therapy. The theory was that if a few people repeated infantile crawling or swimming with David's limbs, that the nerve endings and connections would grow back to their original state.

The problem was not broken bones or crushed limbs, but that the connection between David's head and body was totally severed. Since he was not able to respond or move at all, the doctors were not able to ascertain whether David was even cognizant or aware of anything. He could not even blink his eyes. The laid him on a bed where he stared straight in the overhead lights, which eventually burned his retinas and caused him to become blind. He could not chew, so they fed him with a tube directly to his stomach. They massaged his stomach area to allow his digestive system to function properly. David could not even lick his lips, and they would become parched, and crack and bleed.

We would roll him over on his face on a narrow table, his face munched down into the leather pad. A man would grab each dangling appendage and start the swimming, crawling motions that his therapy consisted of: left arm up, right let up, left leg up, right arm up, over and over again. Men from our church did this for one hour a day, three or four times a week, in shifts and teams. David was not part of our church family, but his nurse Pat was so close to us and so concerned for David that we decided to try to help him.

I went in one day and the doctor was in the hall outside

David's room. His back against the wall, he looked extremely disturbed. Noting the tortured look upon his face, I asked the doctor what was troubling him. His response shocked me.

He said, "If I could take a gun and shoot David dead and kill him, I would." I asked what in the world was wrong.

The physician explained that men had come from Chicago the previous week and tested some new neuro-surgical type of equipment. They put electrodes down into David's head to see if there was a type of brain activity present. Unable to respond by blinking an eye or squeezing a hand, the doctors had assumed that David could not hear or even think, that he was a vegetable. So they inserted electrodes into his head to monitor the readings for several days to find out exactly the extent of David's mental ability.

The doctor was reading the equipment in an area next to David's room, making notes on the data in David's chart, when suddenly all the dials flashed far over into a red area and the monitors began to hum. This was unusual, and the physician went to look in the window of David's room.

David's wife had just walked into the room and said, "Hi, David. How are you?" His two boys briskly flashed by the bed, "Hi, Dad. His Dad," and then sat at a nearby table and did their homework.

When the doctor entered the room, the wife was talking to an aide, "This man does not know who I am. I am lonely and my husband is as good as dead to me. I know I am his wife and I want to be faithful, but my husband has been gone for six years, lying here in this place. I don't have any more feelings toward this person before me. I am going to file for divorce and find someone else who can help me raise my children.

The doctor said the machine hummed and the dials hung on red for hours before they started quivering back down. The doctor now knew for certain, for the first time in six years, that there was nothing wrong with David's mind. His understanding and mental faculties were aware of his situation, but his body would not receive any instructions from his head.

The Father's Voice

There is nothing wrong with the mind of Christ. The Father's mind works perfectly. This God can, with the spittle of His lips, span the darkness of a night's sky with billions upon billions of brilliant stars and galaxies without end. This God breathes, and the winds blow and the waves stir. There is nothing wrong with the mind of a God who can speak and the morning breaks, who takes the evening sky as a pillow to lay the blazing sun to rest. This God created everything from the vastness of the ocean to the height of the mountains to the depths of the valleys. He created bleak deserts and lush rain forests; rocky shores and fruitful plains. There is nothing wrong with the mind of a God whose power stretches through hundreds of billions of star systems. Even at the very edge of revealed space, the creative voice of God may be yet echoing life into the void of nothingness.

There is nothing wrong with God's mind. He just cannot seem to get response from His Body. His Body does not listen to the directions from His Head. There is a disconnection somewhere.

After reading the previous chapters and grasping the truth of the absolute necessity of father-and-son relationship, there is a tendency to hungrily seek a father. With misplaced zeal some launch into a shopping spree for spiritual fathers, improperly pursuing headship. Some look to the person under whose ministry they were initially converted, as their father in the gospel. Others pursue directions unauthorized by the Spirit, endeavoring to be joined to an organizational structure or denominational headquarters in lieu of father covering. Still others wander the aisles of the charismatic smorgasbord with empty carts and checkbook in hand, looking for brand names in colorful packaging.

The truth is that fathers are not chosen from directories or bought from catalogues. A spiritual father is not found by tracing back your spiritual genesis to the one whose ministry brought you to Christ. A father is not chosen from your favorite selection of teachers and preachers who were a great source of help in your life. The ability to speak eloquent words or share information is not the foundation of a father-and-son relationship. Sonship is not predicated on the capriciousness of man, but on the voice of God.

A spiritual father is someone whose life and ministry raised you up from the mire of immaturity into proper growth and order. A spiritual father is the one whose words pierced beyond the veneer of a blessing into the very heart and marrow of your existence, causing massive realignment to your spirit. A spiritual father is not necessarily the one who birthed you into the Kingdom. Instead, he is the one who rescues you from the doorstep of your abandonment and receives you into his house, gives you a name, and makes you his son.

Too many men and women of God have been born into the Kingdom without any spiritual father and live as orphans. Many denominations and ministry fellowships have become huge organizations developed to take care of these spiritual waifs. These orphans are fed, clothed, housed, and educated

The Father's Voice

by systems of men, not raised by fathers. These ministry orphans do not have a name of their own. They carry no spiritual heritage. Many bear the shame of illegitimacy, never being sure of their origin. They are ignorant of their identity and lack clear purpose because it is impossible to know where you are going unless you know from where you have come. So, lacking a true spiritual center, these orphaned people are released upon the stoop of an unwelcoming world. It is because we have not many fathers.

Jesus did not begin His ministry until the voice of the Father was spoken in the earth. "And lo a voice from heaven, saying, This is My beloved Son, in whom I am well pleased." (Mt. 3:17). This is how a father reveals his relationship with a son in ministry. It is the voice of the father that declares sonship. The voice of the father must be spoken, heard, and received in order to establish a father-and-son relationship.

The Spirit of God is sending out a cry. It is a spiritual transmission that declares "the heart of the fathers shall turn to the children, and the heart of the children to their fathers, lest I come and smite the earth with a curse" (see Mal. 4:6). This is a cry of the Spirit that "proceedeth from the Father."

One radio can receive many types of signals. From Bach to Bon Jovi, from sports to news to the proclamation of the gospel—they can all be heard through the same receiver. In the same way that one radio can be tuned to several stations, so we can receive many types of messages from the same Spirit of God.

By the one Spirit we are not only brought to the Kingdom of God, but also given daily direction. "For as many as are led by the Spirit of God, they are the sons of God" (Rom. 8:14).

By the one Spirit, the father-and-son relationship is acknowledged. "The Spirit itself beareth witness with our spirit, that we are the children of God" (Rom. 8:16).

Our spirit receives the message, and the Spirit of His Son in our heart declares our adoption: "...ye have received the Spirit of adoption, whereby we cry, Abba, Father" (Rom. 8:15).

This same voice of the Spirit proclaims our relationships to each other, bearing witness to the connection between father and son in the ministry. Just as we know our heavenly Father by the witness of the Spirit, so we know our ministry father by the one and same Spirit.

The same Spirit that unites us to our heavenly Father will bring us in relationship to our ministry father. If we seek to locate our connection in the Spirit for ministry, we will find our way by the cry of the Spirit. The Holy Spirit "who proceedeth from the Father" bears witness to sons the identity of their father in the ministry (see Jn. 15:26; Rom. 8:16). We must hear the voice of God's Spirit if we desire to connect with our ministry father.

How will we know when and where we are to call out "my father" or receive men as "my sons" in the ministry? Spiritual knowledge is more than a feeling or a strong emotional bonding. It is a sure declaration of the will of God. We must be sure that we hear the voice of the Father in Heaven before we acknowledge fatherhood in ministry on earth. Any claim of ministry connection in the order of father and son must be tried in the courtroom of our spirits.

God Himself spoke His testimony upon the witness stand, "bearing witness" of fathers, sons, and legal heirs. To verify the testimony of any witness as true in a court of law, the witness must take an oath. Before God took the witness stand and declared His Word into the earth, He first took an oath:

> *For when God made promise to Abraham, because He could swear by no greater, He sware by Himself, saying, Surely blessing I will bless thee, and multiplying I will multiply thee. And so, after he had patiently endured, he obtained the promise. For men verily swear by the greater: and an oath for confirmation is to them an end of all strife. Wherein God, willing more abundantly to shew unto the heirs of promise the immutability of His counsel, confirmed it by an oath: That by two immutable things, in which it was impossible for God to lie, we might have a strong consolation, who have fled for refuge to lay hold upon the hope set before us* **(Hebrews 6:13-18).**

The veracity of the testimony of the Spirit is based upon the strength of His oath. In a court of law we take an oath on a Bible, which represents our submission to something greater than ourselves. God can, "swear by no greater" so He speaks a promise and swears an oath on His very own Person.

God will speak the promise to Himself in the heavenly realm and then speak to the person receiving the promise on earth. This is the meaning of the "two immutable things": a promise spoken to those on earth and an oath made to Himself in Heaven.

God will speak "once in the heavens" and "once in the earth." Whenever God speaks a sovereign word in the earth, He does not speak it just once, but twice. When God's voice needs to be heard at a time of great transition, our heavenly Father will call the man on earth not once, but twice. That is why, if God ever does a mighty and glorious turn from Heaven to the earth, He will speak what I refer to as the "Double Enunciation of Deity."

If He wants to change the course of Abraham's obedience and rescue the promise of God, He will not just say, "Abraham" once, but will speak his name twice: "Abraham, Abraham" (Gen. 22:11). If God wants to call a deliverer to rescue His enslaved people, He will say, "Moses, Moses" (Ex. 3:4). When the Lord desires to raise up a pure prophetic voice in the midst of a corrupt priesthood, He calls, "Samuel, Samuel" (1 Sam. 3:10). When the temple is rebuilt after years of captivity God instructs Zerubbabel to install the headstone with the cry of "Grace, grace" (Zech. 4:7).

When the Word made flesh brings forth the word of His Father, He does not say "verily" once, but 25 times in the Gospel of John Jesus says "Verily, verily." When the Savior prays for an "about-to-be-sifted" apostle, He says, "Simon, Simon" (Lk. 22:31). When Jesus appears to a Pharisee gone mad, He says, "Saul, Saul" (Acts 9:4). When God claims someone as a child of the Kingdom, He sends His Spirit into his heart to cry the double name: "Abba, Father." In Heaven and in earth, the witness of God is given by His voice.

This double enunciation of Deity almost always happens in situations where there is no natural answer or where the natural flow is broken. Thus there are times when God sovereignly takes over both positions in a connection. The heavens and the earth are connected by one voice. God speaks in Heaven and earth and says "Abraham, Abraham" because the circumstances were out of control. There was no way Abraham could understand why God would want a human sacrifice, and then not want one. Unless alignment with the Father in Heaven was made with Abraham sovereignly by God, his seed of promise would die.

There is no way Saul of Tarsus would be saved without someone presenting Jesus to him. Without a sermon or a Bible, without illustrations, introductions, three songs and a poem, a murderous Pharisee lies upon his face, struck to the ground by the double enunciation of "Saul, Saul." God made the connection Himself; once in the heavenlies and once in the earth.

At Shiloh is a priestly system that God is weary of, procreating only iniquity and unrighteousness in the "sons of Belial." When an Eli produces a Hophni and a Phineas who steal glory, God will intervene. It is really not understandable, but God will allow a token son to sleep in the back room of his house, a son given away by his own mother out of a prayerful and starving situation in which she made a promise. He is there to receive God's voice.

Before the light goes out in the house of God, the Word of the Lord comes to the boy and cries, "Samuel." Three times the voice cries out his name once: "Samuel." Eli finally recognizes this Voice that has been veiled from him, and instructs the young man to receive revelation. When the voice of God finally calls for recognition and

Samuel says, "Speak, Lord," you will notice God said, "Samuel, Samuel" (see 1 Sam. 3:1-10).

In the earth Samuel could not recognize the heavenly voice. That is why he answered to Eli and not to the Lord. That is what happens so often when men hear the voice of God. They go back to the system and ask, "Is this God?" They go back and ask a failed priesthood, "What am I supposed to do?" It is only when the voice of the Father says sovereignly, "Samuel, Samuel," that the rare voice of God is heard.

Once in Heaven, once on earth; once in transmission, once in reception: The voice of the Father thunders into your spirit and you know it is a connection from God. This is a spiritual knowledge. It is not based on what you know or where you've been, what their names are, how great they are, or how well they are understood. It is the voice of the Father that takes over both sides of the divide and forms a spiritual bridge, spanning the yawning emptiness of man's ability with the purpose and power of God.

The Bible calls these "immutable things," for when you hear that voice, you know you can't be lied to; God cannot lie (see Tit 1:2). If you hear the witness of one, it may not be the truth. But in the witness of two everything is established (see Mt 18:16).

This explains why Jesus said what He did:

If I bear witness of Myself, My witness is not true. There is another that beareth witness of Me; and I know that the witness which He witnesseth of Me is true. ... And the Father Himself, which hath sent Me, hath borne witness of Me. Ye have neither heard His voice at any time, nor seen His shape. And ye have not His word abiding in you: for whom He hath sent, Him ye believe not (**John 5:31-32; 37-38**).

In another place, this conversation took place:

The Pharisees therefore said unto Him, Thou bearest record of Thyself; Thy record is not true. Jesus answered and said unto them, Though I bear record of Myself, yet My record is true; for I know whence I came, and whither I go; but ye cannot tell whence I come, and whither I go. Ye judge after the flesh; I judge no man. And yet if I judge, My judgment is true: for I am not alone, but I and the Father that sent Me. It is also written in your law, that the testimony of two men is true. I am one that bear witness of Myself, and the Father that sent Me beareth witness of Me. Then said they unto Him, Where is Thy Father? Jesus answered, Ye neither know Me, nor My Father: if ye had known Me, ye should have known My Father also (**John 8:13-19**).

The religious folk of Jesus' day did not understand Jesus' identity because they did not hear the voice of the Father. They had "neither heard His voice at any time, nor seen His shape." They could not see the Word made flesh because they could not hear the word from Heaven. They refused the word of the King and His Kingdom connection in their failure to receive the word proceeding from the Father. Even though Jesus did great miracles right before their eyes, they could not receive Him as God because the word was not abiding in them. Even the testimony of two is not enough for those who refuse to hear. Therefore Jesus says 15 times in the Gospels and the Revelation: "He who has ears to hear, let him hear."

The foundation of authority for Jesus' ministry was the voice of the Father. Jesus does not receive the confirmation of men as the basis of His authority. Jesus does not even rest upon His own pure, singular testimony. The Father speaks the Word from Heaven and confirms that Jesus is "the Word made flesh" manifest on the earth. The voice of the Father is the authoritative connection between God and man. This connection only occurs when the voice from Heaven is spoken and heard on the earth. The testimony of two is the basis of all Kingdom possibilities and relationships.

Jesus' ministry did not begin with the heralding of angels and the kneeling of shepherds. His ministry did not start with the amazed gasp of rabbinical scholars who listened to a 12-year-old boy in the temple. The fulfillment of His purpose was not initiated with the acclaim of family and friends who recognized that great gifting and power lay dormant within His bosom.

No, the catalyst for the induction into ministry for Jesus was the voice of His Father:

> ***Now when all the people were baptized, it came to pass, that Jesus also being baptized, and praying, the heaven was opened, and the Holy Ghost descended in a bodily shape like a dove upon Him, and a voice came from heaven, which said, Thou art My beloved Son; in Thee I am well pleased* (Luke 3:21-22).**

This word propelled Jesus into His ministry. He also received this word while He was praying (see Jn. 12:28). The basis of praying in the Kingdom is "in earth as it is in heaven." The "proceeding" word of the Father was heard from Heaven on the earth. Jesus founded His ministry on the testimony of His Father. Without the voice of the Father, Jesus would have stayed in the carpentry shop, sawing trees instead of dying on one.

You will know the voice of a father in ministry because he will speak a "proceeding" word. A father has such a word in his mouth because he keeps a "proceeding" relationship with the Lord. In other words, this word must be progressive enough that it does not get stuck somewhere in a son's maturation process, or keep him short of his potential. This is the voice of true spiritual ordination. This is the word that "proceeds" you into maturity as a son, so you in turn can eventually become a father to others.

A proceeding word is a word from the heart of God.

But those things which proceed out of the mouth come forth from the heart... **(Matthew 15:18).**

The proceeding word is immutable and cannot be argued with or denied.

Then Laban and Bethuel answered and said, The thing proceedeth from the Lord: we cannot speak unto thee bad or good **(Genesis 24:50).**

A proceeding word makes you realize that anything earthly will never satisfy, but only "every word that proceedeth out of the mouth of the Lord" (Deut. 8:3).

A proceeding word destroys satanic attack.

But He answered and said, It is written, Man shall not live by bread alone, but by every word that proceedeth out of the mouth of God **(Matthew 4:4).**

The proceeding word is one like that of the two witnesses in Revelations:

And if any man will hurt them, fire proceedeth out of their mouth, and devoureth their enemies: and if any man will hurt them, he must in this manner be killed **(Revelation 11:5).**

The proceeding word is from God's throne.

And out of the throne proceeded lightnings and thunderings and voices... **(Revelation 4:5).**

God's throne is the proceeding source of flowing impartation.

And he shewed me a pure river of water of life, clear as crystal, proceeding out of the throne of God and of the Lamb **(Revelation 22:1).**

A proceeding word is a word that establishes sons in the Kingdom.

And when thy days be fulfilled, and thou shalt sleep with thy fathers, I will set up thy seed after thee, which shall proceed out of thy bowels, and I will establish his kingdom **(2 Samuel 7:12).**

The proceeding word is the sword of the Lord that cuts through to your soul.

...which sword proceeded out of his mouth... **(Revelation 19:21).**

For the word of God is quick, and powerful, and sharper than any twoedged sword, piercing even to the dividing asunder of soul and spirit, and of the joints and marrow, and is a discerner of the thoughts and intents of the heart **(Hebrews 4:12).**

The Greek word here for "word" is *rhema*. It refers not only to the general body of the inspired Scriptures, but also to a specific, penetrating word of God that brings dynamic, structural change to a person's life. This proceeding word distinguishes between soulish and spiritual connections, and brings us together "bone to bone" in the joints and marrow of spiritual realignment and relationship.

Jacob's experience gives us a picture of the power of the proceeding word. Jacob, alone by the ford Jabbok, which means "flowing, or proceeding" is jumped in the dark by a man who wrestles with him all night. Jacob had no idea who this person could be. He wasn't hairy enough for Esau (not many were). Neither was he trying to kill Jacob, at least not right away. Jacob was a fighter, though, and did not give up. Jacob did not know who he was wrestling with until "...he touched the hollow of his thigh; and the hollow of Jacob's thigh was out of joint, as he wrestled with him" (Gen. 32:25). It was when he was touched in his joint that Jacob knew he was wrestling with God, and asked for a blessing.

A spiritual father will have this proceeding *rhema* word in his mouth. It will perform spiritual surgery and place you out of joint in your present walk with God. This is only so you will be placed in proper order. The "Jabbok" word proceeding from his mouth will change your walk, your name, and your life. Then the spiritual children who proceed from your ministry will bear the name and legacy of that one proceeding word. "Therefore the children of Israel eat not of the sinew which shrank, which is upon the hollow of the thigh, unto this day: because he touched the hollow of Jacob's thigh in the sinew that shrank" (Gen. 32:32).

Hearing the voice of the Father and speaking His proceeding word into the earth is the rock upon which the Church is built.

> ***And Simon Peter answered and said, Thou art the Christ, the Son of the living God. And Jesus answered and said unto him, Blessed art thou, Simon Barjona: for flesh and blood hath not revealed it unto thee, but My Father which is in heaven. And I say also unto thee, That thou art Peter, and upon this rock I will build My church; and the gates of hell shall not prevail against it* (Matthew 16:16-18).**

Simon's name is changed to "rock." Now, Peter is not the foundation of the Church. His name is changed because, like Jacob, Peter received the proceeding word from the Father. Simon will no longer be known by his earthly father (BarJona), but by relationship to his heavenly Father. It is the "Father which is in heaven" whom Jesus states to be the source of this revelation. Simon received the proceeding word, not from men, but from God.

The circumstances surrounding the receipt of the proceeding word dictate the change of the person's name. Abram is renamed "Abraham" because he proceeds from being a father in the spirit to being a "father of a multitude." Jacob changed from being a deceiver to one who "prevails or wrestles with God." Simon, which means "hearing," is called "Peter" because he not only can hear the voice of the Father, but will also speak it upon the earth. The immutable word from the Father makes mountains from men. The gates of hell cannot withstand the proceeding word of God.

This is the key to the Kingdom: "And I will give unto thee the keys of the kingdom of heaven: and whatsoever thou shalt bind on earth shall be bound in heaven: and whatsoever thou shalt loose on earth shall be loosed in heaven" (Mt. 16:19). The original language here literally says this: "Whatever has already been" either bound or loosed in Heaven, shall be bound or loosed on earth. This connection between Heaven and earth is our ability to hear the voice of our Father in Heaven and the proclamation of what the Father is saying on the earth. Thus we pray "in earth, as it is in heaven."

Until we receive that word from Heaven into our world, we will never know our father in the ministry. Sons will not recognize their spiritual father by organizational alliance or personal history. A ministry father is recognized by the "proceeding word" of God within his mouth.

In the prophet Ezekiel's experience in a valley of dry bones, we see the power of the voice of God in connecting together relationships for ministry. Ezekiel was instructed by God to prophesy upon these bones: "So I prophesied as I was commanded: and as I prophesied, there was a noise, and behold a shaking, and the bones came together, bone to his bone" (Ezek. 37:7). The bones were just gathered together until the word from God that assembled the bones proceeded out of the mouth of the prophet. The Church is the Body, the bone structure, of Christ. Until we hear the proceeding word from Heaven, we will remain a grotesque gathering of disconnected body parts.

Today, amid the loud noise of busy churches and filled conferences, there needs to be a shaking and coming together, "bone to his bone." The reason we have such ogre-type ministries and deformed spirituality is because we are not properly connected to our Head and with each other. We must be linked together "bone to his bone" specifically by the voice of the Spirit in functional relationship to one another.

Paul writes that by speaking the truth in love to one another, this "bone to bone" relationship that dictates placement, alignment, and energy within the Body of Christ, comes and grows together:

> ***But speaking the truth in love, may grow up into Him in all things, which is the head, even Christ: From whom the whole body fitly joined together and compacted by that which every joint supplieth, according to the effectual working in the measure of every part, maketh increase of the body unto the edifying of itself in love*** **(Ephesians 4:15-16).**

This "increase of the body" occurs in relationships joined together as we speak to each other. This increase occurs when we find our bones by the voice of the Spirit.

Besides at the baptism of Jesus, the voice of the Father was heard at another time in His ministry. In the fourth Gospel, Andrew and Philip meet a group of travelers identified as "Greeks" who desired to see Jesus. No doubt they had heard of His miraculous ministry and powerful teaching, and not knowing if they would ever be so close to Jesus again, these Greeks said, "Sir, we would see

Jesus." Jesus never gives a direct response to their request; instead, He immediately starts proclaiming truth:

And Jesus answered them, saying, The hour is come, that the Son of man should be glorified. Verily, verily, I say unto you, Except a corn of wheat fall into the ground and die, it abideth alone: but if it die, it bringeth forth much fruit He that loveth his life shall lose it; and he that hateth his life in this world shall keep it unto life eternal. If any man serve Me, let him follow Me; and where I am, there shall also My servant be: if any man serve Me, him will My Father honor. Now is My soul troubled; and what shall I say? Father, save Me from this hour: but for this cause came I unto this hour. Father, glorify Thy name. Then came there a voice from heaven, saying, I have both glorified it, and will glorify it again. The people therefore, that stood by, and heard it, said that it thundered: others said, An angel spake to Him. Jesus answered and said, This voice came not because of Me, but for your sakes. Now is the judgment of this world: now shall the prince of this world be cast out. And I, if I be lifted up from the earth, will draw all men unto Me" **(John 12:23-32).**

Jesus does not really pay these Grecian seekers much attention, but rather breaks into a Gethsemane-type prayer referring to the stormy days ahead that have already begun to stir the waters of His soul. Jesus prayed when He was in the Jordan with John, and the Father spoke at His baptism of water (see Lk. 3:21-22). Now facing a baptism of death, burial, and resurrection, Jesus prays again. Facing the cross and having to bear the world's sin, Jesus calls to the Father to glorify His name. This is when a voice from Heaven declares that God has glorified His name in Heaven and will now glorify His name on the earth as well. God speaks the same word twice: a double enunciation of Deity.

Notice how this spiritual transmission was received. The crowd of witnesses was split in how they heard the voice of the Father. Some said it was just a natural phenomenon-just thunder. But others recognized that it was a voice from Heaven-perhaps an angel. God is always sending His voice into the world, for the judgment of the world comes by the reception of His voice in the earth. Some will say it thundered. Others will say it was the voice of an angel.

Jesus, in being lifted up, draws all men unto Himself, but not all men follow Jesus. Some say He is just a man, while others say He is God incarnate. When a voice from Heaven is heard, some will not regard the voice as from God and will be judged by how they received the Word of God.

Legitimate ministry is based upon the witness of the fathers and the identification of the sons. To some this sounds like thunder. It sounds to some that "fathers and sons" is just another name for blind submission or egotistical authority-wielding. Some will ignore the voice of the Spirit and continue to live as a law unto themselves—illegitimate ministry giving birth to illegitimate ministry. Some fatherless ministries may not be able to hear because of past offense or abuse. Thus they'll stay within the maximum security of an orphanage system of denominationalism or "independent-ism."

On the other hand, there will also be those who recognize the transmission of the Spirit; their hearts are tuned to what

God is saying. These people will know a heavenly voice when they hear it. It will bear witness with their spirits. Ministries will link together, finding "bone to his bone" connections, discovering who they really are and how they fit in Kingdom relationship. Fathers will turn to sons and sons to fathers when the sound of His voice is heard.

The voice of God is audible within the hearts of those who listen for Him. Sons and fathers will know each other by the cry of their spirits one to another, created by the turning of their hearts together. The lamentation of an impartational void within the hearts of sons will cry out for the flow of spiritual inheritance within the heart of true fathers who seek for a son to receive. This is the "deep [that] calleth unto deep at the noise of Thy waterspouts" that, when received, causes "all Thy waves and Thy billows [to go] over me" (Ps. 42:7). The voice of God flows through the canals of spiritual ears and replenishes the barren understanding of orphan ministries with the flood of Kingdom revelation. It is by the gushing might of spiritual flow and the thirsty beds of parched souls that fathers and sons are known.

They shall come with weeping, and with supplications will I lead them: I will cause them to walk by the rivers of waters in a straight way, wherein they shall not stumble: for I am a father to Israel, and Ephraim is My firstborn **(Jeremiah 31:9).**

This relationship of father and son is not chosen by man, but spoken by God. Elisha was plowing a field, never realizing the potential that he had in God. Suddenly, the prophet Elijah appeared and changed the course of his life forever. A new direction in a new dimension resulted when Elijah placed his mantle upon the shoulders of Elisha. "And he left the oxen, and ran after Elijah, and said, Let me, I pray thee, kiss my father and my mother, and then I will follow thee. And he said unto him, Go back again: for what have I done to thee?" (1 Kings 19:20)

Elijah tells Elisha that he is free to say good-bye to his earthly parents to follow his new spiritual father, adding, "What have I done to thee?" Elijah recognized that his placement as Elisha's spiritual father was not of his own doing. Elijah did not choose Elisha; God did. Elijah just obeyed the heavenly voice that said Elisha "shalt thou anoint to be prophet in thy room" (1 Kings 19:16).

The voice of God that called Elisha into the ministry was received when Elijah stood upon a mountain before the Lord.

And He said, Go forth, and stand upon the mount before the Lord. And, behold, the Lord passed by, and a great and strong wind rent the mountains, and brake in pieces the rocks before the Lord; but the Lord was not in the wind: and after the wind an earthquake; but the Lord was not in the earthquake: and after the earthquake a fire; but the Lord was not in the fire: and after the fire a still small voice **(1 Kings 19:11-12).**

God wanted to communicate with Elijah, so He first sent elemental forces that obeyed His command. The wind, earthquake, and fire were not sent to inform or instruct. God sent the strong wind to break anything in the way that could stop Elijah from hearing the voice of God. Likewise, an earthquake served to shake loose any obstruction. The fire was sent, not to tell anything to Elijah, but to burn away any blockage left from the wind or the earthquake.

The Father's Voice

All these things came to Elijah to prepare him to hear the still, small voice of God. The Lord will rarely shout or scream. If His voice is to be heard, fatherly patience is necessary to receive it. Following the process of hearing the proceeding word is essential to being a father in the ministry.

Elijah was not the active agent upon Elisha's life; it was the voice of God that did the calling. Elijah was simply the manifestation of spiritual headship that Elisha submitted to and served as a son. The spiritual relationship between father and son in ministry is the work and choice of God.

There are spiritual fathers yearning to hear from God and looking for where they can cast their mantle. Sons are wanting to acquire fathers, but this relationship is not based on the work of man. My spiritual father is not who won me or taught me. He is not who organized me or who gives me the greatest political platform. My father is not the one who gives me the sweetest fellowship, or the person whom I like to be with the most. Literally, my father is someone who speaks the word that puts me into a position in maturation to fulfill my fullest spiritual potential in God.

So I may have had 10,000 instructors in Christ who brought me to a point, but suddenly, there must be a voice, an impartation, that plunges me into purpose. That is how I will know who my father really is. It will be the "deep calling unto deep" in our lives.

The connection of fathers and sons in the ministry begins in the voice of the Father. This voice of the proceeding word is an impartation of the Spirit. It's like a flash of light against a film negative in a camera. It leaves an impression that is never lost. It actually takes a picture. Through the voice of a father on earth transmitting the proceeding word, this voice of God speaks to me and portrays to me that this is who I am. This impartation gives me a picture of who my father is and what I can become in God.

This word also unites you in process with someone. Jesus says, "If any man serve Me, let him follow Me; and where I am, there shall also My servant be: if any man serve Me, him will My Father honor." (Jn. 12:26). In other words, "If you want to see Me, you must go through My process. I will stamp this image on you just like it is on Me. Where I am, there will you be, honored by the Father." Whenever we join in a spiritual relationship, there is both benefit and baggage interspersed between the parties of covenantal bonds. Whatever process or problems that either person may bring into the relationship must be entered and endured by both. Fathers and sons in the ministry are joined and connected together in an ebb and flow of both life and death. This is a "bone to his bone" connection. If there is health or sickness in either, it is shared by both. When an injury occurs in one bone, all the bones connected to it feel the same pain. A refusal to stay joined in a God-ordained relationship will amputate you from Kingdom purpose.

God has established the order of father and son. He ordained fathers to be an earthly confirmation and witness to the heavenly voice of Father God. Elisha will never be more than a plowboy until Elijah sets his mantle upon him. Saul will forever search for his father's donkeys until Samuel anoints him and he is changed into another man. David will tend sheep and sing songs his entire life until Samuel covers his head in oil, making it ready to wear a crown. John the Baptist would have followed in Zacharias' footsteps as a son of Aaron, sacrificing lambs and filling lamps with oil-except for a proceeding word from an angel that literally turned him into "a voice...crying in the wilderness, Prepare ye the way of the Lord!"

From the heavenly Father to earthly fathers to sons, the voice of God will be heard.

The voice of the proceeding word of the Father to Mary was the connection that formed the ministry of John the Baptist:

> ***"And the angel came in unto her, and said, Hail, thou that art highly favored, the Lord is with thee: blessed art thou among women. And when she saw him, she was troubled at his saying, and cast in her mind what manner of salutation this should be"* (Luke 1:28-29).**

Mary was staggered by the words of the angel. She wondered what such a greeting could possibly mean. The angel told her that she would have a son and that He would sit on the throne of David.

> ***Then said Mary unto the angel, How shall this be, seeing I know not a man? And the angel answered and said unto her, The Holy Ghost shall come upon thee, and the power of the Highest shall overshadow thee: therefore also that holy thing which shall be born of thee shall be called the Son of God* (Luke 1:34-35).**

When Mary responded to the angel with "Be it unto me according to thy word", sonship was conceived in her womb by the Holy Spirit. She received the word of the Father.

Mary not only received the voice of the Father for herself, but the power of God traveled through her voice when she greeted her cousin Elisabeth.

> *And Mary arose in those days, and went into the hill country with haste, into a city of Juda; and entered into the house of Zacharias, and saluted Elisabeth. And it came to pass, that, when Elisabeth heard the salutation of Mary, the babe leaped in her womb; and Elisabeth was filled with the Holy Ghost: and she spake out with a loud voice, and said, Blessed art thou among women, and blessed is the fruit of thy womb. And whence is this to me, that the mother of my Lord should come to me? For, lo, as soon as the voice of thy salutation sounded in mine ears, the babe leaped in my womb for joy. And blessed is she that believed: for there shall be a performance of those things which were told her from the Lord* **(Luke 1:39-45).**

Mary greeted Elisabeth in the form of a salutation, just as the angel had greeted Mary. The power of this salutation was the proceeding word from God that flowed down upon Mary. From the angel, the word came unto Mary, into her womb, and then into Elisabeth and down into her womb. This proceeding word caused Elisabeth's baby to leap within her. It was the proceeding word in the voice of the salutation of Mary that triggered this holy flow of divine power and quickened John the Baptist while still beneath his mother's flesh.

Elisabeth cries out, "And blessed is she that believed: for there shall be a performance of those things which were told her from the Lord" (Lk. 1:45). Elisabeth understood that her barrenness was removed and that life was now leaping in her womb only because Mary received the proceeding word of God.

If Mary had not received the voice of the Father, there would be no Jesus in the world. If there was no Messiah, there would be no need for His forerunner to be born. The spiritual connection between John the Baptist and Jesus would never have occurred if Mary had not received the angelic visitation and proceeding word from the Father. At the voice of Mary's salutation, the power of the Holy Spirit flowed with her words: from God-to an angel—to Mary—to Elisabeth. The leaping baby within her bore witness to Elisabeth that the promise of God was alive on the earth.

Elisabeth and Zacharias were unable to have children, and in her body she was past the time of her womanhood. But because Mary was willing to bring forth Jesus, God smiled upon Elisabeth and she brought forth "the greatest born of woman," John the Baptist (see Mt. 11:11).

Elisabeth might have spent her entire life in the shadow of an empty womb if Mary had not received the proceeding word. Because Mary believed, Elisabeth was blessed and the performance of God's word to her came to pass.

There are sons today ready to be birthed into ministry. Their desire for Kingdom reality has opened the womb of spiritual possibility. They are ready to be formed into anointed vessels to herald the Christ. But the life of God and the anointing of the Spirit has not yet come upon these sons in fullness because someone over them in the Lord has not responded to God's voice.

Unless a father responds to the voice of Father God, sonship will not manifest on the earth. Without the voice of the earthly father, ministry lies dormant within the belly of possibility. A son can be perfect in form and fully knowledgeable of his purpose, but live completely paralyzed by the lack of a father's voice to bring life and anointing.

The cry within the hearts of sons is for a connection with their fathers. It is the cry of the Spirit and the witness of the Spirit that causes the gift of God within sons to leap and come alive. It is the proceeding word that connects power to purpose and anointing to ability in the life of a son in ministry. In receiving the voice of the father spiritual sons become the divine connection for succeeding generations in God.

And thou shalt remember all the way which the Lord thy God led thee these forty years in the wilderness, to humble thee, and to prove thee, to know what was in thine heart, whether thou wouldest keep His commandments, or no.

Deuteronomy 8:2

Chapter 7

The Father's Maturation

On the way to a hostile desert, a fighter pilot holds his position just outside enemy territory and waits for his orders to proceed.

He has been sent on a dangerous mission that not many could survive.

Even with his extensive training and proven ability, the odds are against him without the guidance of a perfect plan.

The seconds seem like hours in this process. He hears nothing.

The radio is mute and the silence is a black as the night around him.

It is here where fear begins to invade and temptation moves in by stealth. A deterring voice disguised as reason:

What are you doing here?

Why are you waiting to receive orders that could send you to your death?

For what reason? Certainly not for the money. A commercial airline would pay you much more, and it's safe.

It couldn't be for fame or recognition. Your battle here is secret. Whether you fail or succeed, become martyr or hero, no one will ever know.

Why are you still here when you could save yourself?

The questions create a great pressure of emotion within the cockpit.

Surrounded by controls of power, he has never felt so weak.

With just one move, he could abandon his position here and use this jet to be anywhere in the world.

Yet the young airman keeps his position with the perspective of a heavenly view and waits for his call to come through.

It is the confirming voice of his commander that reassures him and sends him ahead into the war.

With the coordinates of his destiny, the way has been made clear to pursue his purpose:

Destroy the stronghold of the enemy

And set the captives free.

It is a mission that cannot be completed alone. Only as a member in this great air force.

The Father's Maturation

Can he hope to achieve a purpose and a plan that is higher
Than he could ever reach
In a jet.

The Gospel of Mark records, "And there came a voice from heaven, saying, Thou art My beloved Son, in whom I am well pleased. And immediately the Spirit driveth Him into the wilderness" (Mk. 1:11-12).

Israel is a fertile land of abundant agriculture. It has a moderate climate and beautiful mountains. Winding through its countryside is the Jordan River where the ministry of John and the ministry of Jesus met in baptism. The water was still fresh on the face of Jesus when the Holy Spirit descended. In Jesus' appearance, He looks like His mother Mary, but when the voice of God speaks from the heavens, Jesus is undeniably God's Son.

God, having introduced the greatest ministry that would ever be, now sends His Son into the desert where the only thing as intense as the heat is temptation. However, there is no temptation that is greater than God. So we follow, without fear, into the "process of wilderness."

It is the process of wilderness that heightens our desire for growth and intensifies our desire to be filled. It is the howling of its loneliness that makes us hungry for the presence of God. It is also where satan tempts us with a mirage. He tries to make us veer off course and change direction to a road of good intentions. It is a dry and dusty dead-end street that leads you out of process and away from the purpose of maturity in God.

The first leading of the Spirit in the ministry of Jesus was into the desert God sent His Son into the wilderness of process to prove Him. The evil one met Him there to sift Him.

The Father's Maturation

The Father sends His children into testing to prove their excellence. The enemy sees that testing as an opportunity to cause the failure of sons.

The essence of the wilderness experience is the testing of our relationship with God. It is here that we learn we will never be powerful enough to fulfill Kingdom purposes or resist satanic attack without total submission to God. That submission is the first step a son will take in the maturing process of developing a father's heart.

If satan can stop the process of maturation within a son in the ministry, then he does not have to deal with a father in ministry later. The tactic of the enemy is to abort the child before it can ever reach maturity. Pharaoh killed all male babies so he would not have to deal with a Moses. Herod killed all male babies in Bethlehem so he would not have to deal with another King. The enemy still seeks the death of sons in the process of their development, before they can ever reach their full potential.

The temptation Jesus experienced in the wilderness was directed at how He would exercise the power of His office. The main thrust of attack was on how Jesus would use the anointing He received from His Father. Like the pilot in the beginning story of this chapter, the temptation is to use your given power without proper authority. Would Jesus, now that His Sonship was established and His anointing received, use His position as Son for anything outside the will of the Father?

While Jesus was in the wilderness, satan came to Him. "And when the tempter came to Him, he said, If Thou be the Son of God, command that these stones be made bread. But

He answered and said, It is written, Man shall not live by bread alone, but by every word that proceedeth out of the mouth of God" (Mt. 4:3-4). Jesus was tempted to use His power to feed His starving flesh without a word from the Father.

Jesus is tested next by the suggestion that He throw Himself down from the pinnacle of the temple.

> **Then the devil taketh Him up into the holy city, and setteth Him on a pinnacle of the temple, and saith unto Him, If Thou be the Son of God, cast Thyself down: for it is written, He shall give His angels charge concerning thee: and in their hands they shall bear thee up, lest at any time thou dash thy foot against a stone (Matthew 4:5-6).**

This is not a temptation to commit suicide. Both Jesus and satan know that angels obey the Lord's every command (see Mt. 26:53). The issue here is whether Jesus will use His anointing to gain a large following and total social acceptance from the religious community by performing a miracle at their most prominent, communal location. This would have removed the operation of the Kingdom from a spiritual realm to a natural realm of men accepting men. Jesus would have won men to Himself, not to the Father.

The third temptation concerned the ability to rule the world and have every want or desire met for the rest of your life. The process of the cross would have been rendered unnecessary by a small, unknown, unseen act of submission to an authority that was rejected by the Father. "Again, the devil taketh Him up into an exceeding high mountain, and sheweth Him all the kingdoms of the world, and the glory of

The Father's Maturation

them; and saith unto Him, All these things will I give Thee, if Thou wilt fall down and worship me" (Mt 4:8-9).

Jesus always listened to the voice of His Father. Economic supply, social acceptance in the religious community, and rulership of wealth and power were offered to Jesus in lieu of the father-and-son relationship. In the wilderness, Jesus used the voice of the Father in His counteroffensive against this satanic opposition. When the enemy sought to entice and confuse, Jesus just quoted the progressive word that His Father had spoken: "It is written, Man shall not live by bread alone, but by every word that proceedeth out of the mouth of God"; "It is written again, Thou shalt not tempt the Lord thy God"; and "Get thee hence, Satan: for it is written, Thou shalt worship the Lord thy God, and Him only shalt thou serve" (see Mt. 4:4,7,10).

These are wilderness words. Every statement Jesus quoted here is from Deuteronomy. Jesus, in the wilderness, quoted the Word of His Father that was written, tried, and proven pure in the wilderness of Moses. Jesus carried the voice of the Father with Him into the wilderness.

This is always the defense tactic of wilderness warfare that sons of a father use. This is the advice Paul gave his son in the ministry, Timothy: "Unto Timothy, my own son in the faith.... This charge I commit unto thee, son Timothy, according to the prophecies which went before on thee, that thou by them mightest war a good warfare" (1 Tim. 1:2,18). It is the remembrance of the words of your father as you go into the heat of battle that gives you the strength and authority to return victorious.

There are some things that cannot be learned in the process of formal education and that cannot be attained by generational impartation. You can go to every school in the country and stand in every prayer line until your head is rubbed raw, but you will never learn or receive from them what the wilderness experience will give you. The spirit receives an impartation with the voice of the Father; however, the heart must be in a position of obedience for the power of God to be funneled into Kingdom purpose.

Jesus was put into proper position by the wilderness. "Though He were a Son, yet learned He obedience by the things which He suffered; and being made perfect, He became the author of eternal salvation unto all them that obey Him" (Heb. 5:8-9). Before Jesus can ever call disciples or work a miracle, He must go through the wilderness. Before He ever ushers men into the Kingdom, He must endure the desert. This desert experience was to fulfill the potential of His ministry. Even though He was a Son, He had to go through a process of spiritual development.

Jesus was in the wilderness for 40 days, a recurring time period in the Bible as the number of days necessary for fullness of qualification. The world was not completely flooded until 40 days of rain and gushing springs were released upon the earth. Jacob's embalming and Goliath's taunting both lasted 40 days (see Gen. 50:3; 1 Sam. 17:16). Both Moses and Elijah fasted for 40 days. Israel, in searching out the potential for a victorious conquest, sent 12 spies into Canaan for 40 days. Israel did not fulfill its wilderness period until 40 years had passed, one year for every day that the spies searched the land. Jesus too must spend 40 days in

The Father's Maturation

the wilderness to fulfill the spiritual pattern through His obedience-what they were unable to accomplish because they refused to hear the voice of the Father.

This process is not simply a passage of time, but a period of growth in every area of a son. Joseph's wilderness in Egypt prepared him to rule in wisdom. "He sent a man before them, even Joseph, who was sold for a servant: whose feet they hurt with fetters: he was laid in iron: until the time that his word came: the word of the Lord tried him" (Ps. 105:17-19). The word proceeding from the Father made the determination of Joseph's heart to obey God stronger than the iron that kept him bound. The word will always be tested. It will try you and prove you to be all that the Father said you were.

Joseph spent 17 years in slavery and in prison before the visions of his youth were fulfilled. Jacob spent 20 years in service to Laban before he returned to the land of his bought birthright David first killed a lion and a bear before he ever slew Goliath. David then served Saul as an armor bearer before he ever became Saul's son. David carried armor before he wore the crown.

This period of growth in a son is necessary for him to fully develop so he can receive his inheritance. "Now I say, That the heir, as long as he is a child, differeth nothing from a servant, though he be lord of all; but is under tutors and governors until the time appointed of the father" (Gal. 4:1-2). The order of father and son includes a period where the son ministers as a servant. That is the only way a son develops the servant heart of a father.

The prominent role of service in the process of sonship

is most clearly seen in the relationship between Elijah and Elisha. Immediately upon receiving the touch of Elijah's mantle, Elisha has a big barbecue and a good-bye celebration: "And he returned back from him, and took a yoke of oxen, and slew them, and boiled their flesh with the instruments of the oxen, and gave unto the people, and they did eat Then he arose, and went after Elijah, and ministered unto him" (1 Kings 19:21).

Ministry relationship is often tested. Elisha will meet with this type of relationship test when he serves Elijah. Three times Elisha is tried with the temptation to stop following his father in the ministry: "Tarry here, I pray thee; for the Lord hath sent me to Bethel...to Jericho...to Jordan." Elisha passed each test with his love and response of endurance: "As the Lord liveth, and as thy soul liveth, I will not leave thee." (See Second Kings 2:2,4,6.)

Years pass and mantles shift. When King Jehoshaphat is allied with kings of Israel and Edom, their armies are without water and languish seven days' journey from any source of renewing their supply.

> *But Jehoshaphat said, Is there not here a prophet of the Lord, that we may inquire of the Lord by him? And one of the king of Israel's servants answered and said, Here is Elisha the son of Shaphat, which poured water on the hands of Elijah. And Jehoshaphat said, The word of the Lord is with him...* **(2 Kings 3:11-12).**

Elisha had the most powerful anointing upon his life that any man ever received. He did mighty miracles, raised the dead, and came the closest in similarity to the

The Father's Maturation

miraculous ministry of Jesus than any other Old Testament man of God. Yet Elisha is not recognized as a great prophet or a great preacher, but as a great servant who "poured water on the hands of Elijah." Service is the road to greatness for "he that is greatest among you shall be your servant" (Mt. 23:11). The memory of Elisha is always acquainted not only with great miracles, but most prominently with the loyal service of a son to a father.

Before Jesus hears the voice of the Father and is cast out into the wilderness to begin His ministry, we see Him at 12 years old, teaching in the temple. Robed rabbis with long beards and phylacteries stand with mouths wide open in amazement at the wisdom of this youth. For three days and nights He taught the Sadducees and Pharisees, until they are totally in shock. He took care of all His physical needs while He was there: food, shelter, clothes, money, etc. He was able to live on His own.

This is the greatest teaching gift around! Jesus was fully aware of who His father is, who He is, and the purpose in His life. "...How is it that ye sought Me? Wist ye not that I must be about My Father's business?" (Lk. 2:49). Young Jesus was fully able to minister then.

Yet, Jesus will return with Joseph and Mary. "And He went down with them, and came to Nazareth, and was subject unto them: but His mother kept all these sayings in her heart And Jesus increased in wisdom and stature, and in favor with God and man" (Lk. 2:51-52).

It will be 18 years before the verbal river of grace pours from His lips in the temple again. It was the 18 years of ministry silence that prepared Jesus. Submission to

Joseph and Mary was necessary in order for Jesus to listen for the voice of His Father. Without this process, He would not have been qualified in sonship.

Some will go through a process of growth. Others will go through a process of service; while still others will simply wait until their time is fulfilled. Some may even go through a process of a literal wilderness. The point is not the necessity of suffering; all people suffer at some time or another. The period of time between "the cross and the crown" was so maturity could take place within the heart of a son.

Moses lived for 40 years in the backside of a desert before he became the deliverer of his people. Egypt can train you to be a leader of men, but only the wilderness can teach you to be a man of God.

The place of preparation for John the Baptist was not in the marbled floors of Herod's temple. Nor was his reflection often seen in the shiny brass of the brazen altar. To find John, you had to go somewhere else besides the pinnacle of religious success. "And the child grew, and waxed strong in spirit, and was in the deserts till the day of his shewing unto Israel" (Lk. 1:80); "Annas and Caiaphas being the high priests, the word of God came unto John the son of Zacharias in the wilderness" (Lk. 3:2).

When God decides to crack the silence of 400 years with a prophetic voice, He will not speak through the normal and accepted religious channels. A corrupted high priest, one who had sold out for the porridge bowls of personal profit, will not speak for God. When God wants to herald the coming of the Messiah, He will not choose polished voices and trained choirs. God will choose "the voice of one crying in the

The Father's Maturation

wilderness, Prepare ye the way of the Lord" (Lk. 3:4).

John the Baptist came from the wilderness. He was so led by the voice of the Lord that when asked about his identity, he could only describe himself as the voice of God. "Then said they unto him, Who art thou? that we may give an answer to them that sent us. What sayest thou of thyself? He said, I am the voice of one crying in the wilderness, Make straight the way of the Lord, as said the prophet Esaias" (Jn. 1:22-23).

It will be in the ministry of John the Baptist that "the hearts of the fathers [turn] to the children, and the disobedient to the wisdom of the just; to make ready a people prepared for the Lord" (Lk. 1:17). The process of maturation is necessary for sons in the gospel. It is the only way that they can ever become fathers.

The Lord does not look at the wilderness in the same way as we perceive it. Jeremiah tells us that the Lord compares the wilderness to a honeymoon with His Bride:

> *Moreover the word of the Lord came to me, saying, Go and cry in the ears of Jerusalem, saying, Thus saith the Lord; I remember thee, the kindness of thy youth, the love of thine espousals, when thou wentest after Me in the wilderness, in a land that was not sown* **(Jeremiah 2:1-2).**

God sees our time in the wilderness as a beginning. It was in the wilderness that the people of Israel received the "daily bread" that their fathers had never known. No other generation saw the pillar of cloud by day and the pillar of fire by night. Waters flowed from a rock when they were thirsty. Their clothes and shoes did not wear out for 40 years. In the wilderness the people of God established a priesthood, built a tabernacle, and heard the voice of God. In the wilderness, Moses veiled his face because the glory of God was so strong at times that his face glowed from His presence. The wilderness was a place of divine supply and powerful visitation. It was also the place where an entire generation was taken to die. The honeymoon was over when they disobeyed God's voice.

The temptation to reject the voice of the Father is the essence of the testing of relationship in the wilderness. Jesus was assaulted by the enemy about the very word of the Father: "This is My beloved Son, in whom I am well pleased" (Mt. 3:17). The enemy first comes to Jesus and asks "If thou be the Son of God...." The attack from satan will always come on the heels of revelation because he becomes extremely nervous when the voice of the Father is manifested in the earth. He knows the power of sonship.

The Church of the New Testament had to contend with certain evil spirits that specifically targeted the maturity of sons in the ministry. "Woe unto them! for they have gone in the way of Cain, and ran greedily after the error of Balaam for reward, and perished in the gainsaying of Core" (Jude 11). Please notice how these failures of promise are grouped together: Cain, Balaam, and Korah. These are the names of three men in the Old Testament who failed to properly mature in the process of their lives. They are mentioned again in the New Testament because they are more than men who once lived. These three surface in the Church as representing major spirits that seek to take the heart of a son away from a father. They bear the names of men in the Bible who were gifted, but who used their abilities for selfish gain instead of for Kingdom purpose. These spirits seek to eliminate maturity in a son of the gospel so he can never become a father to others. They seek to abort the mission of the son before his ministry is ever launched. The spirits of Cain, Balaam, and Korah target sons in ministry to destroy their potential in the Kingdom. Every true son in the ministry must pass through all three of these attacks on their way to becoming fathers in the ministry.

Cain will murder his brother: "For this is the message that ye heard from the beginning, that we should love one another. Not as Cain, who was of that wicked one, and slew his brother. And wherefore slew he him? Because his own works were evil, and his brother's righteous" (1 Jn. 3:11-12). The spirit of Cain in a member of the family of God drives him to not want anyone to have more of the Spirit than he himself has. The spirit of Cain in him burns with anger and assassinates the character of anyone who is accepted and received more than he. Cain must be first, and nothing is more important to him than his preeminence.

This is false maturity. Whenever this spirit is in a man and he sees someone more righteous or greater than himself, he will hate that man. The spirit of Cain will not allow his life to change in the light of a greater example. Rather, he will do everything in his power to destroy anyone greater, until nothing greater than himself exists. He will strive to be the greatest. In short, all he ever does is compare himself with others and eliminate all his competition. Cain cannot accept a brother who has a greater gifting or ability than himself. He will kill him, and so destroy his own potential in the same act.

Balaam gave some of the most powerful prophecies in the Bible. But he also sold out his calling and used his gifting to increase his fortunes and turn the hearts of Israel to sin. Balaam was led astray from maturity by the potential in his gifting. Balaam could have joined the Israelites in their journey. He saw the beautiful tents of Israel, but realized he could obtain more wealth if he looked somewhere else besides the Lord for supply. The world sought to use his gifting from God for their own purposes. Balaam reached out for two worlds, and lost them both.

Balaam, himself gone astray, leads sons of Israel astray while they are maturing in the wilderness. He cannot curse them, so he perverts them and causes many to never enter the promise of their fathers. Though Balaam the man perished long ago, the spirit behind him lives in the Church today:

> ***But there were false prophets also among the people, even as there shall be false teachers among you, who privily shall bring in damnable heresies, even denying the Lord that bought them, and bring upon themselves swift destruction. ... Which have forsaken the right way, and are gone astray, following the way of Balaam the son of Bosor, who loved the wages of unrighteousness; but was rebuked for his iniquity; the dumb ass speaking with man's voice forbad the madness of the prophet* (2 Peter 2:1, 15-16).**

This spirit will also be in the church in Pergamos: "But I have a few things against thee, because thou hast there them that hold the doctrine of Balaam, who taught Balac to cast a stumblingblock before the children of Israel, to eat things sacrificed unto idols, and to commit fornication" (Rev. 2:14). Pergamos represents one of seven types of churches today. The spirit of Balaam is alive and visible, selling revelation for profit and seducing hearts of men away from the Father. Yet, "The Lord knoweth how to deliver the godly out of temptations, and to reserve the unjust unto the day of judgment to be punished" (2 Pet 2:9).

Korah will perish because of "gainsaying." This word in the Greek is *antilogia,* the combination of *anti,* as in *antichrist,* and *logos,* which is the Greek word used to refer to Jesus as the "Word *[logos]* made flesh." To "gainsay" is to speak "words against the word" that has been given.

Those who perish in the way of Korah speak evil words to come against the word that was given. They are described in the Book of Jude: "Likewise also these filthy dreamers defile the flesh, despise dominion, and speak evil of dignities. ... These are murmurers, complainers, walking after their own lusts; and their mouth speaketh great swelling words, having men's persons in admiration because of advantage" (Jude 8,16).

The sons of Korah will be swallowed up because they sought to use their gifting to elevate their position.

> *Now Korah...took men: and they rose up before Moses, with certain of the children of Israel, two hundred and fifty princes of the assembly, famous in the congregation, men of renown: and they gathered themselves together against Moses and*

> *against Aaron, and said unto them, Ye take too much upon you, seeing all the congregation are holy, every one of them, and the Lord is among them: wherefore then lift ye up yourselves above the congregation of the Lord? And when Moses heard it, he fell upon his face* **(Numbers 16:1-4).**

A revolt broke out in the deacons of Israel, turned against Moses and Aaron by the sons of Korah. They felt that the senior pastor, Moses, and his brother, Pastor Aaron, were just not quite the type of leadership that men of their caliber deserved.

These men wanted to go back to Egypt. Bondage to an evil system was preferred over bondage to someone whom they saw as their equal in authority. They saw Moses as a brother, not as a father. They based this attitude on the fact that they too were gifted as Moses and Aaron were. These deacons in the wilderness considered their gifting to be a source of leadership. They confused a gift of power with the mantle of authority.

God gives powerful gifts to His Body, but "power gifts" are not given so the recipient can rule over set authority. Gifts are given for horizontal edification, exhortation, and comfort—to build up the body. They are never for the qualification for leadership.

Men are set in headship positions as fathers in the ministry because of their heart and ability to receive from the Lord. This heart for the Father is the qualification for headship, regardless of whether or not they have powerful giftings.

Many pastors and leaders may have less gifting in certain areas than do the people they lead. The ability or gifting to teach, prophesy, or manifest power does not make someone

The Father's Maturation

the leader of God's people. That is why Paul wrote the verse used as theme of this book: "I write not these things to shame you, but as my beloved sons I warn you. For though ye have ten thousand instructors in Christ, yet have ye not many fathers: for in Christ Jesus I have begotten you through the gospel" (1 Cor. 4:14-15). He was warning them not to substitute gifting for being a father in the ministry. This is the major test of potential sons in the ministry.

This is the trap that many churches fall into, especially when the set ministry of a local church encourages the development of the people to become everything they can be in God. A pastor with the heart of a father will be willing to decrease in his operation of gifts, and will refuse to completely overshadow his sons. He does so to give room for the burgeoning growth of sons under him in the ministry. He bends back his limbs so that the saplings beneath him can grow into stately oaks and towering pines. This is the joy of being a father in the gospel.

This can also become the source of great wounding and the spring from which the tears on a father's face flow in the night seasons of his soul. His decrease, out of love for his spiritual offspring, can become the fuel of their rebellion. The situation that a father too often finds is that out of his heart for the Kingdom develops the very monster that steals half his congregation and uses them to start another church down the street The reason the rebelling son of Korah usually gives is that the gift within his rebellious heart is "too big" for the limitations he felt under the father who gave the people everything. These men and women are children who cannot submit to fatherly leadership and so remain in immaturity.

It is the recipe of rebellious sonship to make stones into bread to feed the hunger of self. The typical response of their departure is, "God is leading me to somewhere else." What they mean is: "This is not what I wanted, so it must not be God." They have been overcome by the hatred of Cain. They were waylaid by the ways of Balaam. They were swallowed up in the gainsaying of Korah. What ministries they could have had! What mantles they may have worn! What blessing was lost with them!

Their names are a Rogues Gallery, echoing through the ages, from the Old Testament to the New Testament and beyond. The seed of Canaan will never bring honor to their father. The cries of Esau are heard howling in the tents of Isaac, birthright sold, blessing gone. Having stolen gold and garments, Gehazi traded his legacy for leprosy. Judas sold his apostleship, only to buy his burial plot. Demas loved this world, and lost his soul.

Reuben, as the firstborn son, lost his double-portion inheritance from Jacob because he slept with the concubine of his father. The last words Jacob spoke to him from his deathbed were, "Reuben, thou art my firstborn, my might, and the beginning of my strength, the excellency of dignity, and the excellency of power: unstable as water, thou shalt not excel; because thou wentest up to thy father's bed; then defilest thou it: he went up to my couch" (Gen. 49:34). Both of Joseph's sons will head a tribe, and Judah will birth a Christ. But the tribe of Reuben will disappear.

Absalom took his father's kingdom. "...When any man came nigh to him to do him obeisance, he put forth his hand,

and took him, and kissed him. And on this manner did Absalom to all Israel that came to the king for judgment: so Absalom stole the hearts of the men of Israel" (2 Samuel 15:5-6). He died, caught in the snare of pride and rebellion. This is the end of those who seduce men away from their father in ministry.

In Deuteronomy 8, we are told that God sent the Israelites into the wilderness and allowed them to hunger only so He could feed them. The reason so many ministries today experience personal wilderness and ministry barrenness is not because God wants them hungry. It is because He wants to provide bread from Heaven. This is bread that they do not find in the comfort of plenty. "And He humbled thee, and suffered thee to hunger, and fed thee with manna, which thou knewest not, neither did thy fathers know; that He might make thee know that man doth not live by bread only, but by every word that proceedeth out of the mouth of the Lord doth man live" (Deut 8:3).

Do not curse your wilderness. It is the place where sons become fathers.

And the holy garments of Aaron shall be his sons' after him, to be anointed therein, and to be consecrated in them. And that son that is priest in his stead shall put them on seven days, when he cometh into the tabernacle of the congregation to minister in the holy place.

Exodus 29:29-30

Chapter 8

The Father's Garments

He stood at the edge of Egypt waiting for 75 men, women, and children to appear on the horizon. Joseph clutched his linen tunic, rubbing the inlaid jewels and twisting the gold threads woven throughout his garment. He remembered another cloth long ago ...

He was given a coat of many colors, a coat of favor from his father Israel. To wear your father's love, to feel his covering upon your skin ... Joseph would trade the finest robe in Egypt for that coat, if only he could wear it again.

His brothers had also felt his coat — as they ripped it from his shoulders. Naked and screaming, Joseph was carted off to slavery, his garments in sodden strips on the ground. His brethren covered the stain of their sin with the blood of a goat, clothing themselves in deception.

Joseph would wear other coats, but he would never lose the love of his father, nor the favor of his God. A Hebrew slave became the overseer of Potiphar's house, only to have another ferment torn from his shoulders. Again his covering was removed and used against him as a cloak of falsehood, his honor taken to shield the dishonorable.

Chained in a prison uniform, the blessing of Jacob's God was still unfettered in the life of his son. Through the dreams of a baker and cupbearer, the dreams of Joseph would prove to be true.

Robed in the finest of Egypt and with the authority of Pharaoh, Joseph searched the horizon before him once again, looking for his final desire to be fulfilled. Soon he would look on the face of his father. Joseph, in a short time, would place his arms around the man who gave him everything. Wait ... there were dots on the desert. A caravan from Canaan, and the one in front was limping.

The Father's Garments

Jacob gave his son a covering of authority and favor made with the materials of love, effort, and time. Joseph filled it with honor and faithfulness. It is a woven picture of the relationship between father and son.

Many seek the power of the anointing without the garments of a father. They are unable to function in true spiritual authority because they are not properly clothed. Garments in Scripture are a type that give us a picture of the spiritual inheritance from father to son. The order of father and son in the line of Aaron clearly demonstrates the need for spiritual garments.

> *And Aaron and his sons thou shalt bring unto the door of the tabernacle of the congregation, and shalt wash them with water. And thou shalt take the garments, and put upon Aaron the coat, and the robe of the ephod, and the ephod, and the breastplate, and gird him with the curious girdle of the ephod: and thou shalt put the mitre upon his head, and put the holy crown upon the mitre. Then shalt thou take the anointing oil, and pour it upon his head, and anoint him. And thou shalt bring his sons, and put coats upon them. And thou shalt gird them with girdles, Aaron and his sons, and put the bonnets on them: and the priest's office shall be theirs for a perpetual statute: and thou shalt consecrate Aaron and his sons* **(Exodus 29:4-9).**

Notice that while Aaron is anointed, his sons are not. They are given coats. Sons of Aaron were not themselves anointed at the inception of ministry. Aaron alone had the oil poured upon his head. The only anointing that the sons received was by the impartation of the anointing contained in the garments of their father. The point of this passage is the absolute necessity of the generational connection that must exist for proper perpetuation of ministry. Garments are created to contain the anointing and to cover the flesh of the ministry. They serve as containers that hold the inheritance from father to son in ministry.

> *And the Lord spake unto Moses and Aaron in mount Hor, by the coast of the land of Edom, saying, Aaron shall be gathered unto his people ... Take Aaron and Eleazar his son, and bring them up unto mount Hor: and strip Aaron of his garments, and put them upon Eleazar his son: and Aaron shall be gathered unto his people, and shall die there. And Moses did as the Lord commanded: and they went up into mount Hor in the sight of all the congregation. And Moses stripped Aaron of his garments, and put them upon Eleazar his son; and Aaron died there in the top of the mount: and Moses and Eleazar came down from the mount* **(Numbers 20:23-28).**

The anointing was passed from this father to his son by the oil captured in the garments of the high priest and by the son's receiving the garments upon the father's departure. The firstborn or elder brother of Aaron's sons would receive them as an inheritance.

This truth is so vital. Although we have desperately sought the anointing, we have not been properly clothed to receive it, nor correctly garbed to perpetuate generational connection and inheritance. The people of

God have been so busy living in single generational pursuits that they have only single-portion anointing. The anointing is placed on the flesh of those who pray and receive. However, since there is no garment, the fragrance and essence of the oil soon dissipate, and there is never any flow to the next generation. As a result, each new generation of ministry must begin at the genesis of impartational development and hope they live long enough to reach revelation.

This is why we need fathers in the ministry. A father must clothe his sons in the gospel with his love, encouragement, and support. Then not only is the gift of the father extended beyond his own heartbeat, but sons can then minister as well. If they are uncovered and un-anointed, it is the result of not having many true fathers. The hearts of fathers must turn. We must make "garments of praise" for our sons, and refuse to die without imparting our anointing.

> *And take thou unto thee Aaron thy brother, and his sons with him, from among the children of Israel, that he may minister unto Me in the priest's office, even Aaron, Nadab and Abihu, Eleazar and Ithamar, Aaron's sons. And thou shalt make holy garments for Aaron thy brother for glory and for beauty. And thou shalt speak unto all that are wise hearted, whom I have filled with the spirit of wisdom, that they may make Aaron's garments to consecrate him, that he may minister unto Me in the priest's office* (Exodus 28:1-3).

Here we see the institution of a fivefold ministry: Aaron and his four sons. We understand that the basis of this ministry is to be a son of Aaron. The very first thing that God requires about the ministry of a priest is the creation of holy garments. Why? The only way that the anointing can ever "be an everlasting priesthood throughout their generations" (Ex. 40:15) is by creating a garment to capture the anointing of the father.

Without a garment, a generational work of God cannot be accomplished and the anointing will become an exhibition of the flesh. "...This shall be an holy anointing oil unto Me throughout your generations. Upon man's flesh shall it not be poured..." (Ex. 30:31-32). The anointing must not touch the flesh of the priests. Ministry cannot be anointed in its flesh. Garments were created to contain the anointing that was poured down upon Aaron so his sons could also receive the anointing.

As the garments were handed down from father to son, the anointing would soak into the fabric. The garment would receive the oil of each high priest, over and over through each passing generation. Saturation would be generationally increased. The anointing was increased, and the fragrance enriched "throughout their generations."

We could have greater anointing flowing in our lives. Jesus said we would do "greater works than these" (Jn. 14:12), yet we see very little of what the early Church had in abundance. We lack power because we lack garments on the body to capture and contain the anointing. We lack garments because "we have not many fathers."

We have gone outside the order of God. We have lost the pattern for garments and so cut off our generations (see Ex. 30:33). Uniforms of education and denominations wear out. Financial gain, eloquent speeches, or social standing are only fig leaves of man-made design that quickly wither. These are unable to contain oil or leave an inheritance for the next generation.

In order for the saturation of generations to be imparted, a priest must wear the garments of his father.

> *And the holy garments of Aaron shall be his sons' after him, to be anointed therein, and to be consecrated in them. And that son that is priest in his stead shall put them on seven days, when he cometh into the tabernacle of the congregation to minister in the holy place* **(Exodus 29:29-30).**
>
> *And ye shall not go out of the door of the tabernacle of the congregation in seven days, until the days of your consecration be at an end: for seven days shall he consecrate you* **(Leviticus 8:33).**

A son receives the anointing of his father by wearing his father's clothes until the anointing is rubbed into him. The number of days, seven, indicates a completion or level of perfection in the process necessary for consecration unto divine service. As the young priest wore the clothing of the high priest, he would begin to sense the burden that his father carried in the tabernacle of God. He became intimately acquainted with the smell of his father's labor as well as the fragrance of the priestly anointing. The son experienced the inheritance of the blessing and the pain associated with ministry. This would serve to introduce him into both the warmth and the weight of his calling.

A son, in becoming identified with his ministry father, must also become identified with all the father's "baggage."

The history of both good and bad must be borne on the son's shoulders. It is the only way for the identity of fatherhood to rest in his heart. Somewhere in the process of son-ship, the son of the high priest will be seen walking in the same steps, wearing the same garment as his father. Someone will remark, "Is that Aaron or one of his sons? I cannot really tell the difference."

Fathers must provide garments for their sons. They create garments by their "praise" (see Is. 61:3) of the sons' obedient service. Fathers create garments by clothing their sons with honor and support. They allow their sons to "walk in their shoes" of leadership and decision-making for as long as it takes to perfect their sons.

Not only do fathers supply garments for their sons, but through the mutual impartation of covenant relationship, sons must at times cover their father. Noah lay exposed in his tent and Ham gazed with satisfaction and told "with delight" the condition of his father. Shem and Japheth, though, took a garment upon their shoulders and walked backward, keeping their backs to their father because their hearts were toward him, to cover the nakedness of their father. Love covers a multitude of sins (see 1 Pet 4:8), and garments conceal our original state. Noah, naked in his tent, received a garment from his sons to cover his shame. Contained within the cloth was the honor given to a father in the ministry by sons. (See Genesis 9:20-27.)

These garments were more than material sewn with a needle and thread. They were a material manifestation of the lives of fathers and sons that were knit together in the service of the Lord. In the order of father to son is a sharing of life and ministry that is vital to the recovery of generational blessing in the Church. Fathers and sons are connected by the same proceeding word, the same calling and purpose. By their experiences shared together, they are knit together. A mutual impartational flow is established that brings a flow of "spirit to spirit" from a "bone to his bone" connection, which produces generational increase in Kingdom manifestation and character.

Elijah and Elisha were not naturally father and son. Their relationship was based on the spiritual connection of father and son. The voice of God came to the man of God:

> ***And it was so, when Elijah heard it, that he wrapped his face in his mantle.... And the Lord said unto him...and Elisha...shalt thou anoint to be prophet in thy room.... So he departed thence, and found Elisha the son of Shaphat, who was plowing with twelve yoke of oxen before him, and he with the twelfth: and Elijah passed by him, and cast his mantle upon him* (1 Kings 19:13, 15-16, 19).**

Elisha was not anointed with oil. Just like the sons of Aaron, the garment of his ministry father was placed on his shoulders. It was the mantle of a prophet that turned Elisha into a prophet like unto his father. This was the spiritual connection that would change his life forever: He left his natural parents and his following the oxen to follow in the steps of a spiritual father.

Elijah also became more than just a prophet or a teacher. He was the father to Elisha in ministry. Elisha served Elijah in the faithfulness of a son, and when his service of sonship was complete, Elijah asked Elisha,

"Ask what I shall do for thee, before I be taken away from thee. And Elisha said, I pray thee, let a double portion of thy spirit be upon me" (2 Kings 2:96b). (In order to receive the double portion, the father must ask the son, "What would you have me do for you?" If a son asks, "Father, give me mine inheritance," without the prior questioning of the father, he is a prodigal who cares nothing for the father. He only wants to spend his inheritance on himself.)

Elisha received a double portion of Elijah's spirit when his father in the ministry was whisked away in a fiery chariot. "And Elisha saw it, and he cried, My father, my father, the chariot of Israel, and the horsemen thereof. And he saw him no more: and he took hold of his own clothes, and rent them in two pieces!" (2 Kings 2:12). Shedding his own garments, Elisha received the inheritance of his father. Elisha then did the works of his father and rolled back the waters of Jordan by smiting them with this cloak of double-portion containment (see 2 Kings 2:13-14). This mantle was his birthright.

We do not need to pray for anointing. We already have the anointing (see 1 Jn. 2:20,27). What we must do is contain the anointing. This is why garments are not an arbitrary form of inheritance in the Spirit. We cannot minister to a dying world in our flesh. We must have double-portion ministry in the Church. What we need to pray for, is for fathers to make garments for sons to wear. It is their inheritance.

At Jesus' birth, an angelic proclamation declares the means of identifying the Messiah to a small band of shepherds. "And this shall be a sign unto you; Ye shall find the babe wrapped in swaddling clothes, lying in a manger" (Lk. 2:12). From the swaddling clothes of infancy to the brightness of transfigured clothes to the seamless garment of maturity beneath the cross, God can always be identified by His garments.

In Mark chapter 5 we are told of a certain woman who had an issue of blood for 12 years. In speaking to her, Jesus called her "daughter." She was hemorrhaging at the place of intimate relations. This daughter of Zion was unable to have proper relationship; she was incapable of giving birth to sons and daughters. The woman went to physician after physician, spending all her money, but grew worse in her condition.

This woman is a type of the Church. Her 12 years of physical deterioration represent the loss of foundational understanding in the Body of Christ. We have lost the blessing of generational impartation from father to son. Our life is spilling out from us; our identity and relationships are suffering without strength. We go from conference, to conference searching for someone who may have a word or who can give us a sign, but all the while we are hemorrhaging to death, disabled in Kingdom relationships and utterly barren of spiritual offspring. Yet, when the woman with an issue of blood touched just the hem of His garment, she was healed. Unless we have garments, the Church will never contain the power of the Spirit

The apostle Paul also passed the anointing in garments. "And God wrought special miracles by the hands of Paul: so that from his body were brought unto the sick handkerchiefs or aprons, and the diseases departed from them, and the evil spirits went out of them" (Acts 19:11-12).

His containing garment was a handkerchief. This literally was a "sweat rag" used by Paul in his tent-making labors. One person cannot be everywhere. A lot of people in ministry today act as if the anointing of God begins and ends with them. But the anointing and the work in service to Christ is something to be shared. It is not a feeling or an attribute of one person; those things cannot be carried in a cloth. The anointing is of the Spirit and it flows from one person to another in the woven cloths of relationship.

Timothy was so close to Paul, his father in the ministry, that as they labored together, he soaked up the anointing. Then Timothy was set apart and sent like a handkerchief in the hand of God to bandage the wounded and dry the tears of those in a more distant place.

What a tragedy it would be if we thought that the anointing God has given to us should begin and end with us. What a loss it would be if the generation that comes after us are orphaned prophets left behind to watch us depart in a blaze of glory, and to search for a lost father instead of ministering to a lost world.

Let us father sons so that all we have been given in Christ does not die. Let us hand down an inheritance that is a garment of relationship woven in the many colors of grace.

It is like the precious ointment upon the head, that ran down upon the beard, even Aaron's beard: that went down to the skirts of his garments; as the dew of Hermon, and as the dew that descended upon the mountains of Zion: for there the Lord commanded the blessing, even life for evermore.

Psalm 133:2-3

Chapter 9

The Father's Anointing

The minister quietly sat down in his office. He was feeling rather terminal in front of his terminal. The intimidation factor was apparent. It just sat there ... like a one-eyed monster, square and squatting. It waited to shoot our deadly rays to mutate this placid, plump pastoral person into a mad and raving lunatic.

Last week he had all of his notes for the Sunday message typed and spaced out in a font large enough that, when placed on the pulpit, he could read from almost anywhere on the platform. He was almost done with hours of painstaking labor, re-learning old typing skills, stumbling through large-cased letters and semi-colons. He was almost finished with his first gargantuan effort on the computer since he had bought it. He was proud to finally be in the twentieth century of keyboards and computer chips. He was feeling rather hi-tech, suave, and sophisticated when suddenly — a sharp, quick blink on the monitor ... another blink ... kind of a blurt, a buzz ... then nothing but a blank screen.

What was that? Where is the back-up disk? Oh no! Did I not put it in? Aaargh!!

He had assumed that his labor, his work, his sweaty inspiration would not be lost. He thought that he had put the floppy disk in the little slot. He had not. His work was gone ... all gone. He thought it was being saved as he typed. He thought that he was saved until this happened. Is that why they call it a cursor? Lightning, electrical surge, programming glitch, the devil ... whatever had attacked him, it had done its job well. It was gone forever.

The words of his friends swirled in the dazed pastor's mind: "What do you mean you don't have a computer? You could really use a computer, you know. It will be a blessing. Everybody has one. It would be such a big help in your ministry. You need a computer."

Yes, it was such a big help. He did not feel much need right now, except for maybe a baseball bat ... or a gun ... a small explosive device perhaps ...

Well, that was last week. The pastor, fully recharged and repented, returned to his desk that had been taken over by this ... this thing. The icons flashed across his screen and came into focus. The beginning beeps tolled their chimes. The genesis of pastoral frustration began to ring through the speakers on the sides of the monitor. As the computer turned on, amid the whirring of fans and blinking of monitors, the pastor remembered the first time he ever saw a computer.

The year was 1953 and his seventh-grade class had gone on a field trip downtown to the old Mutual Bank building. They had a computer there that was huge. He and his classmates were told it weighted 30 tons and took up four complete stories of the building. There were only about 100 computers in the entire world at that time, and this was one of the latest and best of its kind. They called it a super computer.

The pastor counted back the years on the abacus of his mind, not wanting to believe that was more than 40 years ago. Computers sure had come a long way. From 30 tons to four pounds; from four stories of a building to the inside of a briefcase. They had multiplied from just 100 computers in the world, to hundreds of millions of computers everywhere, in just one generation. Whey they became smaller, they became greater.

The pastor humorously referred to his computer as "the beast", after hearing so many sermons on the antichrist being a computer. The beast that slept on this pastor's desk had a Pentium chip, and zoomed at 120 megahertz with a one-gigabyte hard drive and a tape backup. The six-speed CD Rom and the 28.8 fax modem went well with the 15-inch SVGA monitor and large mounted speakers. He had bought the top of the line.

He had no choice, actually; the computer industry had

grown so quickly from the 286, 386, 486, to the Pentium before him. In just a few years, even this model would be obsolete and would join the heap of other dilapidated machines. If he bought the best now, it wouldn't be obsolete quite so fast.

Yes, he paid thousands of dollars and bought the very best computer he could afford. He armed it with the latest software and placed it on his desk to collect dust until he gathered his courage and sat down in front of it last week. Of course, the way each new generation of processing chip so quickly becomes greater than the previous one, he will have to update soon.

When he lost his notes on the computer last week, he almost lost his sanity and sanctification with it. He had asked his wife how they could send a man to the moon, but not make a computer that worked properly. Of course, his wife reminded him that they sent a man to the moon on much less of a computer than was presently on his desk. She gently added that it was not the computer that forgot to put in the disk. She also reminded her future computer expert that she loved him, and encouraged him to not give up.

So he is back. Cursor to icon, double click of the mouse, and away he went.

The pastor is in the program ... let us pray!

The Father's Anointing

Everything has advanced and grown through the generations. Mankind has exceeded himself in everything he has done: medical breakthroughs, space shuttles, computers, communication, technology, transportation, industry, etc. Everything has gotten better and better. Everything but the Church.

The Church has more people, money, buildings, influence, political clout, and exposure on television and radio than ever before. Yet, we have not equaled the powerful flow of the Spirit experienced in the first generation of the Church. We have been promised in the Bible a much greater abundance of God than we are presently experiencing. Still, we have only stories of a few special meetings or gatherings where the power of God is manifested, and even then never as great as we read in the Bible.

The problem is not God. The apostle Paul prayed that the Church would know "what is the exceeding greatness of His power to usward who believe, according to the working of His mighty power" (Eph. 1:19). God is the God of exceeding greatness. The term *great* means that a certain level has been reached or a specific goal met. Reaching that certain place determines that something is great. For instance, a baseball player is great if he hits the ball over a certain demarcation: the fence. If something reaches a certain point or a particular magnitude that is clearly as good or better than previously known, that is greatness.

God is not just great, He is exceeding in His greatness. He never just reaches that certain level: He always goes beyond what He has done before. God never simply attains a particular place of greatness and then stops. He goes way beyond our ability to even comprehend His greatness. God has not blessed the Church and said, "That is enough. I think the Church has received all the power it needs. It is time to level off and just find some comfortable place to maintain what it has now."

God does not reach a point of excellence and then cease to move beyond that point. God excels beyond the last excellence He manifested. He exceeds His own boundaries, breaks His own records, and reaches beyond His last stretch. He is always exceeding the place He was before. Our God is the God of exceeding greatness (see Eph. 3:20).

The problem concerning anointing in the Body of Christ today is not the lack of power. God is always pouring out His Spirit. Moses said, "...would God that all the Lord's people were prophets, and that the Lord would put His spirit upon them!" (Num. 11:29) God wants His anointing to be poured on every member of the Body, to where "your sons and your daughters shall prophesy, your old men shall dream dreams, your young men shall see visions: and also upon the servants and upon the handmaids in those days will I pour out My spirit" (Joel 2:28-29).

God wants to exceed what He did in the first centuries of the Church today in the last days of the Church. The reason we do not have the power of the anointing as we could be experiencing it is that we are not receiving the anointing properly. God is always pouring out, but we have not positioned ourselves to be fully covered with His power.

The Father's Anointing

In Psalm 133, we have three verses that form the key to understanding the proper flow of anointing in the Body of Christ. They give us a picture of the direction, alignment, and increase of power in the inheritance of anointing.

***Behold, how good and how pleasant it is for brethren to dwell together in unity! It is like the precious ointment upon the head, that ran down upon the beard, even Aaron's beard: that went down to the skirts of his garments; as the dew of Hermon, and as the dew that descended upon the mountains of Zion: for there the Lord commanded the blessing, even life for evermore* (Psalm 133).**

The power of the anointing is based upon the direction of its flow. The direction of anointing is always down. It flows "upon the head," and then "down upon the beard, even Aaron's beard," and still "down to the skirts of his garments" to the hem of the garments of the priest. The direction of anointing is always down. This is the only way the whole body is covered.

Referring to the previous chapter, you remember that the sons of Aaron were not themselves anointed for their ministry. Aaron alone had the oil poured upon his head. The anointing was passed from father to son by the oil captured in the garments of the high priest and by the sons' receiving the garments from their father. The anointing could only come upon the sons in their relationship with the head of the family, Aaron. The firstborn or elder brother of Aaron's sons would receive the garments as an inheritance. This same order was fulfilled in the ministry of Jesus, "the Apostle and High Priest of our profession," and the Church (Heb. 3:1).

The Head of the Church is Christ. The term *Christ* means "Anointed." He is the Head of the Body. "And He is the head of the body, the church.... For it pleased the Father that in Him should all fullness dwell" (Col. 1:18-19). Aaron was anointed upon his head. The Church is anointed only on the Head, which is Christ, the Anointed One.

Aaron did not receive oil anywhere else but on his head. In Psalm 133, the oil was not placed on his arm, or heart, or legs first It was not poured anywhere but on the head. The anointing flows from the head down and covers him all the way to the hem of his garments.

Jesus promised His disciples that the power of the Holy Spirit would be placed upon them when He sent them the promise of the Father: "And, behold, I send the promise of My Father upon you: but tarry ye in the city of Jerusalem, until ye be endued with power from on high" (Lk. 24:49). The word translated as "endued" is from the Greek word *en-duo,* which means: "to place upon (in the sense of sinking into a garment); or to invest with clothing." From the Head of the Church, who is the Christ, comes the anointing upon the Church through the garment of the Spirit provided by the Father. The Church receives power by being clothed with the Spirit of the Father.

Jesus is the Christ He is the One who is anointed, and as members of His Body, we are clothed with His Spirit The Church is the "one new man" and the "one body" by which we have "access by one Spirit unto the Father" (Eph. 2:15-17). There is no anointing outside of connection with Christ. The only anointing that we receive has been poured from the Head upon His Body, the Church. Jesus told us He would clothe us with power, not pour oil on our heads.

The purpose of the anointing is to empower for service. It is to glorify God, not to exalt the flesh. If we are properly clothed, if we have "put on" the Lord Jesus, then the anointing will magnify Him in our lives. If we are properly hidden in Christ, then His anointing will be seen, not us: "But we have this treasure in earthen vessels, that the excellency of the power may be of God, and not of us" (2 Cor. 4:7; see also Is. 52:1; 61:10; Rom. 13:14; Gal. 3:27; Col. 3:12).

What the Church calls "seeking the anointing" is really nothing more than stirring up a gift God has placed within the believer by the Spirit's residence in his life. That is what should be done. Paul encouraged Timothy to do this very thing: "Wherefore I put thee in remembrance that thou stir up the gift of God, which is in thee by the putting on of my hands. For God hath not given us the spirit of fear; but of power, and of love, and of a sound mind" (2 Tim. 1:6-7).

The phrase *stir up* refers to stirring up a fire that is in need of attention before it goes out. It is to re-position logs in the fire and stir dying embers ablaze. This is the maintenance of a gift already placed in us, not the search for any more power from Heaven. God has already given power, love, and a sound mind to the Church. The anointing is not something "sought." It is the stirring up of what we have already received (see Judg. 16:20; 1 Jn. 2:20).

Timothy was told to stir up the gift of God that was in him by the laying on of the hands of his father in the ministry. How we receive gifting for ministry is to be properly clothed and properly positioned beneath the ministry of a spiritual father. Not only do we also receive a spiritual gift in this manner, but we also receive the anointing on a constant basis if we stay in our position. The anointing does not flow up, so lifting ourselves up is not the way to receive the fullness of God's power. The anointing flows down, so we must "go with the flow" to receive.

The apostle Peter said this: "Likewise, ye younger, submit yourselves unto the elder. Yea, all of you be subject one to another, and be clothed with humility: for God resisteth the proud, and giveth grace to the humble. Humble yourselves therefore under the mighty hand of God, that He may exalt you in due time" (1 Pet 5:5-6). This passage does not refer to a person of chronological age; an elder in the Lord is someone with maturity in ministry. The way to become exalted by God is to stay under the hand of the father in the ministry with whom God has placed us. The flow of the Spirit is down. If we go up, we go against the current of God. We encounter God's resistance in this direction: "for God resisteth the proud, and giveth grace to the humble" (1 Pet. 5:5). If we lift ourselves and our personal gifting above the purpose, position, or person that God has placed over us, we remove ourselves from the flow. We might receive the dew of the mountaintop, but we would never experience the mighty flow of a river. We might receive anointing, but we would have no garments to contain it.

"As the dew of Hermon, and as the dew that descended upon the mountains of Zion: for there the Lord commanded the blessing, even life for evermore" (Ps. 133:3). The anointing is always flowing down, so the most powerful flow of the anointing will not be on the head of Aaron, but at the hem of his garment. The most powerful flow of water will not be the dew at the top of Mount Hermon, but the gushing River Jordan that flows down at the foot of the mountain. Mount Hermon rises 9,232 feet above sea level, making it easily the tallest mountain in Palestine. It can be seen from as far away as the Dead Sea, which is 120 miles away. The runoff from its snow-covered peaks provides the principal source of water for the Jordan River.

The Jordan, which flows for 127 miles, is the longest and most important river of Palestine. It rises from the foot of Mount Hermon and flows into the Dead Sea. Its headwaters lie more than 1,000 feet above sea level, and its mouth is nearly 1,300 feet below sea level. Moisture collects and flows southward into the Sea of Galilee. The Sea of Galilee is about 8 miles wide and 14 miles long. At its deepest point the lake is 1,300 feet deep. At the Galilee's southern end, the Jordan exits and flows 65 miles on down to the Dead Sea. The Jordan River empties an average of six million tons of water every 24 hours into the Dead Sea.

All of this water comes from the dew that drops at the top of Mount Hermon. Thus the dew on the mountain becomes the river in the valley. So the greatest thrust of its flow is not at the head, but at the bottom of its reach. The name "Jordan" means "the descender." In order to receive the waters of the Jordan at its most powerful point, one must be positioned at its lowest level. The reason that dew on the top of Mount Hermon can turn into such a powerful, life-giving river is that it goes down.

The woman with the issue of blood in the Gospels did not touch the head of Jesus. She did not grab His hand and stick it on her head to produce a transfer of anointing. She reached out and touched the hem of His garment—and Jesus felt the power flow out of Him. The most powerful flow and containment of anointing is found at the lowest place in the garments of Christ. The greatest power is at the lowest point because of its position in the downward flow; it is at the place of greatest receiving. Position is essential to the increase of power.

The Church has for too long tried to seek the anointing out of proper order. The Bible never tells us to pray for the anointing, to seek the anointing, or to exalt the anointing in order to receive it. Because God is always pouring out His Spirit, position is the key to receiving the anointing. Those who lift themselves above their headship will receive only the dew of anointing. As a result of their inordinate self-exaltation, they place themselves out of position for receiving the flow of tremendous power at the hem of the garment. This is why so many have an anointing, but it is not in the depth, power, or impact of the Church in the Book of Acts.

We are "in Christ." God wants His Church to have everything that He placed in Christ. God is constantly pouring out of His Spirit Jesus Christ is the anointed Head of the Body. The anointing flows constantly from Him to cover the entire Church. Proper positioning of ministry sons and fathers is essential for recovering the flow of the Spirit. There must be fathers turned toward pouring their gifting down into sons, and sons under their hand to receive. The Church is out of alignment for receiving the flow of His fullness because it does not follow the order of father and son. The impartation of the generations merely trickles when it could be a torrential downpour. So we settle for dewdrops of power when we could have an enormous, mighty, gushing river of power flowing on and through every member of the Body.

The order of father and son is not an attempt at elitism within the Body. Nor is it sectioning out only certain people to receive the anointing of the Spirit. It is not an attempt to sever or create a destructive amputation of power. Rather, this book is written because the order of father to son is the way of God for every member to receive the anointing. It is the course by which the anointing is meant to flow. The operation of spiritual gifts should flow freely within the entire Body as He wills.

"It is like the precious ointment upon the head, that ran down upon the beard, even Aaron's beard: that went down to the skirts of his garments" (Ps. 133:2). The anointing must flow down the Body to reach the fullness of coverage that God intended for His Church. The anointing flows down the head to the beard. The "beard" represents the maturity of leadership. Beards are not grown upon children or youths without years. The anointing is not for the infantile movements of an immature Church. It is not for the childish exaltation of individual talent or the premature presentation of personal eloquence. The anointing is to be placed upon mature, full-grown headship in the Church.

The oil then runs down upon the shoulders of the body. This portion of spiritual anatomy represents the fivefold governmental offices of the Church. "For unto us a child is born, unto us a son is given: and the government shall be upon His shoulder: and His name shall be called Wonderful, Counsellor, The mighty God, The everlasting Father, The Prince of Peace" (Is. 9:6). Aaron bore the names of the 12 tribes on his shoulders: "And thou shalt put the two stones upon the shoulders of the ephod for stones of memorial unto the children of Israel: and Aaron shall bear their names before the Lord upon his two shoulders for a memorial" (Ex. 28:12). The Ark of the Covenant was borne upon the shoulders of the priests: "And the children of the Levites bare the ark of God upon their shoulders with the staves thereon, as Moses commanded according to the word of the Lord" (1 Chron. 15:15). The oil first must flow upon the shoulders. Then it will flow down to the rest of the body.

What is true with the body of Aaron is true with the Body of Christ. Christ is the Head of the Church: "...Christ, when He raised Him from the dead, and set Him at His own right hand in the heavenly places, ...and gave Him to be the head over all things to the Church, which is His body, the fullness of Him that filleth all in all" (Eph. 1:20,22-23).

The fivefold offices that are the shoulders of Church government must have mature leaders to bring the Church to a place of maturity.

> *And He gave some, apostles; and some, prophets; and some, evangelists; and some, pastors and teachers; for the perfecting of the saints, for the work of the ministry, for the edifying of the body of Christ: till we all come in the unity of the faith, and of the knowledge of the Son of God, unto a perfect man, unto the measure of the stature of the fullness of Christ: that we henceforth be no more children, tossed to and fro, and carried about*

Head. This is why proper order within the Body is essential for everyone to receive of the anointing in full measure.

Sometimes situations develop in ministry that cause the anointing to flow outside the order of "Aaron and his sons," or the order of father and son. Without relationship in this order of father and son, any anointing to minister will be out of order. It is an illegitimate use of anointing to place personal gifting above order or headship. Neither does the presence of anointing alone qualify someone to minister or govern a congregation. Like a cheap copy of an expensive cologne or perfume, it is a clone, not a natural son that considers having and manifesting a gift in the Spirit as the sole right to ministry. Jesus was gifted, but "...Christ glorified not Himself to be made an high priest; but He that said unto Him, Thou art My Son, today have I begotten Thee" (Heb. 5:5). It was not His gifting that qualified Him, but His submission as a Son.

A generation arose after the death of Joshua that did not "know" the Lord. They were not in relationship with the Lord. "In those days there was no king in Israel: every man did that which was right in his own eyes" (Judg. 21:25). In the Book of Judges, there were several individuals who were anointed by the Spirit during this period of anarchy. They were anointed and raised up to lead the people of God for a short period of time, though never longer than a single generation. Then the people would fall into bondage again, and "corrupted themselves more than their fathers" (Judg. 2:19). The people would cry out to God who, in His mercy, would anoint individuals to lead a generation to freedom again.

Judges like Gideon, Samson, Jepthah and others were mighty in power. They were anointed, but not in the order of father to son. There was no generational blessing. In their day there were no fathers who raised sons in ministry. These judges were raised up by the Lord to become fathers to Israel. None were successful in passing the anointing of God in their lives to the next generation. Although the judges were anointed, it was not the normal or accepted pattern of God. God poured out His Spirit on them because He answered the people's prayer for deliverance. It was His mercy that anointed them, not His approval of their lack of order.

Today there are many people who exercise ministry gifts and have an anointing from God. This anointing is not necessarily an endorsement of their character or their life. After all, Samson slept with Delilah and still had the anointing of the Spirit. Gideon led the people to great victory, and was still anointed when he illicitly made an ephod that caused the people to enter idolatry (see Judg. 8:27). The presence of the anointing is not the qualification for ministry. It is from the Lord, and can be in someone's life outside proper order and relationship (see Mt. 7:21-23; 24:11-12).

The flow of all power in the Kingdom of God is through relationship with one another. The amputation of relationship has left the Church handicapped in power. The disjointed connection in the order of God's people has made some members lame and withered in spiritual atrophy. Other members have become exhausted, overburdened with an unbalanced share of Kingdom responsibility and care. To manifest a complete Christ to the whole world, spiritual connections must be restored and the balance of power shared by each member. Without connection to the perfection of Christ the Head, the Body will remain disjointed, disfigured, and incapable of manifesting the power and image of God in the earth.

The Bible never states that the way to have fullness of the Spirit is through a connection with an organization or denomination. That is headship without relationship and authority without covenant. Neither will the anointing ever reach its fullest level in the Church just by gathering together in huge meetings or local megachurches. The multiplication of anointing is not attained by large numbers of people who have single portions gathered together. That is anointing without covering and power without containment. The only proper channel for the river of anointing from Christ to the Church is from father to son.

> For this cause have I sent unto you Timotheus, who is my beloved son, and faithful in the Lord, who shall bring you into remembrance of my ways which be in Christ, as I teach every where in every church.
>
> 1 Corinthians 4:17

Chapter 10

The Father's Relationship

It is the end of the world, when great men fall.
When men of renown we call "the sons of God"
Disappear.
We looked up to them, those great ones of old.
They were like fathers who put a face on God
With the expression of His Word and power of authority.
Towering high above us, they resembled Deity.
But they were flesh.
Giants in their own eyes, they chose their own way
To cross the line that separated
Night from day.

You Have Not Many Fathers

So, in the height of their greatness
Heaven looked down on them and cried
A flood of tears
When they chose to be intimate with the world,
Aliens to God,
They were reproducing themselves in a continual infancy,
Diluting their future and shrinking their lives
Into extinction
While, in our desperate search for immortals, we overlooks a man
Whose stature of faith was greater
Then mere skeletal frame:
Noah.
He considered his relationship with God
Greater than any beauty man could produce.
He remained faithful to his father
As he groaned and traveled to see
The sons of God on the earth
By building a heritage for us,
His children,
Who live today among the fossil remains of dry bones
And wait for the promise of rain ...

The Father's Relationship

Remembering a man, who,
With obedience, faith, and gopher wood
Built for us
A bridge
That took us from the end of the world
To the beginning of rainbows
(Genesis 6)

Whenever a major truth surfaces within the Body of Christ, a counterfeit of the original will always develop. When God started to speak to the Church again concerning prophets, it seemed everyone turned into a prophet. Recently, much has been said concerning the restoration of apostles in the Church. However, you cannot call yourself to apostleship. Now with the resurgence of the order of father and son in the ministry, many will herald themselves as fathers. They will seek honor that is not their due, and submission that is not their right. They are not true fathers in ministry, but false fathers.

In the time of the judges, the Bible tells us, "...there was no king in Israel, but every man did that which was right in his own eyes" (Judg. 17:6). There are times when God allows a situation of disorder before He brings His people into order. There are times when God winks at ignorance until He requires obedience to revealed knowledge. In the days of the judges, there was a definite lack of godly leadership. The fulfillment of God's pattern for ministry was perverted by the turning of men's hearts toward financial gain instead of fatherhood.

> *And there was a young man out of Bethlehem-judah of the family of Judah, who was a Levite, and he sojourned there. And the man departed out of the city from Bethlehem-judah to sojourn where he could find a place: and he came to mount Ephraim to the house of Micah, as he journeyed. And Micah said unto him, Whence comest thou? And he said unto him, I am a Levite of*

The Father's Relationship

> ***Bethlehem-judah, and I go to sojourn where I may find a place. And Micah said unto him, Dwell with me, and be unto me a father and a priest, and I will give thee ten shekels of silver by the year, and a suit of apparel, and thy victuals. So the Levite went in. And the Levite was content to dwell with the man; and the young man was unto him as one of his sons* (Judges 17:7-11).**

This Levite is a forerunner of a carnal clergy that seeks to "find a place" to operate in their gifting for the sole purpose of monetary gain. This Levite traveled the countryside in pursuit of personal gain and financial fortune. He cared nothing about righteous order or genuine fatherhood. He stayed with Micah because he was hired to be a father. This Levite was not a true father. He was a hired hand, fed and clothed in the house of Micah.

This situation is totally out of order. This is not a picture of a father-and-son relationship. This is a son who makes God in his own image. This is a father who is nothing better than a prostitute. The Levite will perform a task only for the money he receives-and does it in the name of a father.

During this time, the tribe of Dan had not received their inheritance in the land of promise. Without an inheritance of their own, they sent out five men to go and search the land for the inheritance of another. While on their way to conquer Laish, they stopped at Micah's house.

> ***And the five men that went to spy out the land went up... and took the graven image, and the ephod, and the teraphim, and the molten image.... And they said unto [the priest]...go with us, and be to us a father and a priest: is it better for thee***

> *to be a priest unto the house of one man, or that thou be a priest unto a tribe and a family in Israel? And the priest's heart was glad, and he took the ephod, and the teraphim, and the graven image, and went in the midst of the people. So they turned and departed...* **(Judges 18:17,19-21).**

This Levite was not a father or a priest. He was simply a figurehead of religion for hire. When an opportunity for greater wealth and prestige came, he did not hesitate to abandon his previous employer and steal his goods. The people who paid him for his service did so only because he had the proper attire. Dressed for success in the world of empty religion, this Levite was sought by those who saw the material trappings of a priest in an ephod as the sole requirement for ministry.

There are men today in the Church who will enter a city or region and gather together a ministry in the name of fatherhood or apostleship. They will have the right appearance, but they use the garments of priesthood for their personal gain. These men teach the necessity of father-and-son relationship and press the local ministry under their own covering. The stress of the relationship is placed only on the money that must be given to the father in ministry by the sons.

There is no real relationship or true spiritual bonding in that. Honor should be given only to an authentic father in ministry. This sick, perverted counterfeit of a genuine father-and-son relationship is an abomination to the Lord. Before there is ever an exchange of funds from a son to a father, there must be a prior relationship in the Spirit.

The Father's Relationship

The father in ministry is not a hired hand who performs a set task for a certain price. A father is not someone who demands money without a relationship. A father is not someone who seeks to build his own ministry. A father in the ministry is a man of God whose heart is toward raising sons in the gospel, not obtaining servants to rule. A father in the ministry seeks to increase the ministry of sons to the exceeding greatness available in God. A father is identified not by his ownership of an ephod, but by his father's heart, which is turned toward a son.

There will always arise counterfeits to anything genuine. Many times a man or a movement in the Church will begin in original righteousness, only to become a twisted mockery of religious form without substance. At the time of the ministry of John the Baptist and Jesus, there were several diverse groups within the confines of Judaism. Each one represented what occurs when the revelation of God is placed beneath a system where "every man did that which was right in his own eyes" (Judg. 17:6).

During the 400 years of God's silence between Malachi and Matthew, the Jewish religion became corrupt and was mixed with the systems and structures of the world. In the days of Jesus, there were the Sadducees, Pharisees, and Herodians. The Sadducees were the descendants of Aaron; they controlled the priesthood. The Herodians controlled the actual building called "Herod's temple." The house built for God was called by the name of the man who, in his great cruelty and murderous heart, slaughtered the babies of Bethlehem (see Mt 2). The Pharisees controlled the synagogues and exercised great control over the general population.

Each of these diverse groups were the result of a perverted twisting of the order of father and son. The Sadducees were the perversion in the priesthood of Aaron and his sons. The Herodians supported a system that was a perversion in the kingship of David and his sons. The Pharisees in the synagogues were the perversion of ministry fathers in a local setting.

These three groups perverted the order of God and themselves through mixing the revelation of God and the systems of men. They ruined the purity of God's ways by blending them with the tradition of men. Jesus warned His disciples that the ways of the Pharisees, Sadducees, and the Herodians could leaven the whole lump, destroying the simplicity and purity of their relationship with God:

> ***Then Jesus said unto them, Take heed and* beware of the leaven** *of the* **Pharisees** *and of the* **Sadducees (Matthew 16:6).**

> *And He charged them, saying, Take heed,* **beware of the leaven** *of the Pharisees, and of the leaven of* **Herod (Mark 8:15).**

Leaven refers to the permeating influence of a substance that spreads throughout whatever it touches. Leaven is a piece of dough that has within it the yeast that makes the dough rise. It is also what causes the bread to spoil. "A little leaven leaveneth the whole lump" (Gal. 5:9).

Leaven is dangerous because it only takes a small amount of added corruption to ruin the whole loaf. Whenever we begin to place some doctrine of men above the Word of God, we are in danger of the leaven of the

The Father's Relationship

Pharisees. If the office of ministry ever begins to be a place where men appoint men to serve in political positions apart from Kingdom purpose, we are tasting the leaven of the Sad-ducees. Whenever the order of father and son in ministry becomes a role of dictatorial power and subservient obeisance, you have the leaven of Herod. We must return to the simplicity of one loaf of unleavened purity in the Church. Beware of the leaven.

The Church did not begin with huge edifices that point to the sky, or with large organizations ruled by the appointment of men. The Church began with Jesus and His relationship with His disciples. Jesus called 12 men and laid the entire future of the purpose of God into their hearts.

> ***"And He goeth up into a mountain, and calleth unto Him whom He would: and they came unto Him. And He ordained twelve, that they should be with Him, and that He might send them forth to preach, and to have power to heal sicknesses, and to cast out devils"*** **(Mark 3:13-15).**

They were called in this order: First, to be with Him. Secondly, that He might send them forth. Thirdly, that they would have power to heal sicknesses and to cast out devils. This is the relationship of a father to a son.

Jesus was not only the Father manifest in the flesh (see 1 Tim. 3:16), but He was also the father in ministry to the disciples. Their ministry was not birthed in the confines of the halls of academia. Their gifting was not placed upon them in a weekend conference. The foundation of the ministry of the Church is the relationship the disciples had with Jesus.

The Church has swallowed the leaven of production religion. We feel ministry must always be doing something. Yet, Jesus calls us to "be" with Him before we ever "do" something for Him. Although we do not stay in a place of inactivity forever, all relationships begin by simply being together.

The relationship between Paul and Timothy is an excellent example of a father-and-son relationship in the New Testament. The Book of Acts tells us that Timothy traveled with Paul and ministered unto him (see Acts 19:22). As they travelled together, Timothy was able to receive an impartation of the joy and the burden of the ministry of an apostle. He saw how Paul established churches (see Acts 16:4-5), and learned the importance of the leading of the Spirit as Paul sensitively sought direction for ministry (see Acts 16:6-10). From Galatia to Macedonia, to the planting of the Philippian church, through Thessalonica, Berea, Athens, Corinth, and Ephesus, Timothy followed Paul.

The relationship of father and son leads the son to grow in the ministry. Timothy, in a few short, exciting years of ministry, comes alongside Paul and is placed on an equal level to some settings. Notice how some of the epistles are addressed:

> ***Paul, and Silvanus, and Timotheus, unto the church of the Thessalonians which is in God the Father and in the Lord Jesus Christ: Grace be unto you, and peace, from God our Father, and the Lord Jesus Christ*** **(1 Thessalonians 1:1).**
>
> **And sent *Timotheus*, our brother, and minister of God, and our fellow-laborer** *in the gospel of Christ,* **to establish you, and to comfort you concerning**

The Father's Relationship

your faith **(1 Thessalonians 3:2).**

Timotheus **my workfellow,** *and Lucius, and Jason, and Sosipater, my kinsmen, salute you* **(Romans 16:21).**

Paul, and Silvanus, and Timotheus, unto the church of the Thessalonians in God our Father and the Lord Jesus Christ **(2 Thessalonians 1:1).**

Paul, an apostle of Jesus Christ by the will of God, and Timothy **our brother,** *unto the church of God which is at Corinth, with all the saints which are in all Achaia* **(2 Corinthians 1:1).**

Paul **and Timotheus, the servants of Jesus Christ, to all the saints in Christ Jesus which are at Philippi, with the bishops and deacons (Philippians 1:1).**

Paul, an apostle of Jesus Christ by the will of God, and Timotheus our brother **(Colossians 1:1).**

Paul, a prisoner of Jesus Christ, and Timothy our brother, unto Philemon our dearly beloved, and fellow-laborer **(Philemon 1).**

Although he is a son, Timothy is called a workfellow and a brother, and is sometimes placed on the same level with Paul. This is the fruit of the father-and-son relationship. Paul has taken a young man who ministered in a limited field of influence and stretched his potential to limits that would have never otherwise been reached in his life. A father will establish a relationship to a son in ministry that, for that person, will be the beginning in a new path of revelation and maturity. The son matures into more than he ever dreamed possible. The father has done more than simply reproduce his ministry; he has multiplied it.

The relationship of father and son in ministry is the foundation of all ministry. The manifestation of this relationship in ministry reflects the relationship between God the Father and the Lord Jesus Christ, His Son. The following outline demonstrates the dynamics of the father-and-son relationship. There are basic principles that can be seen in the relationships between the Father and Jesus, Jesus and the disciples, and Paul and Timothy.

A. Fathers send sons into ministry.
   1. Jesus is sent by the Father to the world (Jn. 7:28-29; 17:3).
   2. The disciples are sent into the world as the Father sent the Son (Lk. 9:2; Jn. 20:21).
   3. A father in ministry sends his son into ministry (Acts 19:22; 1 Cor. 4:17).

B. Fathers confirm sons in their ministry.
   1. The Father bears witness and confirms the sending of His Son (Jn. 5:37; 8:17-18).
   2. Jesus bears witness and confirms the disciples (Mk. 16:20; Jn. 20:21-22).
   3. Paul bears witness of Timothy's ministry to congregations where he is sent (1 Cor. 4:17; Phil. 2:19-22).

C. To those to whom he is sent, the son will manifest the father in mind, word, and deed.
   1. Jesus manifested the Father.
      a. Jesus followed the will of the Father (Jn. 4:34; 5:30; 6:38).

The Father's Relationship

      b. Jesus spoke the words of His Father (Jn. 7:16,18; 14:24).
      c. Jesus did the works of His Father (Jn. 5:19; 9:4).
      d. Jesus did the works of the Father by the power of the Father (Jn. 14:10).
  2. The apostles manifested Jesus to the world.
    a. The apostles followed the will of God (Acts 5:29).
      b. The apostles taught the words of Jesus (Acts 4:13,18-20; 5:28,42).
      c. The apostles did the works of Jesus (Acts 5:12,41-42).
      d. The apostles did the works by impartation of power from Jesus (Acts 3:12-16).
  3. Timothy manifested his father in the ministry to those whom Paul sent him.
      a. Timothy has the same mind and will of his father (Phil. 2:19-22).
      b. Timothy teaches the ways of his father (1 Cor. 4:17).
      c. Timothy does the works of his father (1 Cor. 16:10).
      d. Timothy has an impartation from his father (2 Tim. 1:2,6).

D. Many who profess to love the father will despise the son.
  1. Jesus was despised because He was sent by the Father (Ps. 22:6; Is. 53:3; Jn. 15:24)

2. The apostles were despised because they were sent by Jesus (Lk. 10:16; Jn. 15:20-21; 1 Cor. 4:9-10).

3. Timothy and Titus were despised because they were sons sent of a ministry father (1 Cor. 16:10-11; 1 Tim 4:12; Tit. 2:15).

E. Those who receive the son who is sent, receives the father who sends him.

1. Those who receive Jesus receive the Father (Jn. 12:4445).

2. Those who receive the disciples receive Jesus (Mt. 10:40; Jn. 13:20).

3. Those who receive Timothy receive Paul (1 Cor. 4:17; 16:10).

You can hear the love of a father in Paul's words as he describes Timothy to the Philippians: "For I have no man like-minded, who will naturally care for your state. For all seek their own, not the things which are Jesus Christ's. But ye know the proof of him, that, as a son with the father, he hath served with me in the gospel" (Phil. 2:20-22). This glowing commendation was the garment on Timothy's shoulders that gave him the freedom to minister to the Philippian church. Some men go all their lives and never hear a word of affirmation from their father. These men never become what they could have been in God.

The confirmation of a father is important for one very simple reason: The flow of authority in ministry is from father to son. Jesus did His ministry under the authority of His Father. He did not testify of Himself. Jesus followed the principle of the testimony of two in His ministry: "If

The Father's Relationship

I bear witness of Myself, My witness is not true" (Jn. 5:31); "I am one that bear witness of Myself, and the Father that sent Me beareth witness of Me" (Jn. 8:18).

The son in ministry should not bear witness of himself. The flow of authority is breached by that action. Whatever words or actions a ministry does to place itself or exalt itself into a certain position is not in order. It causes harm to both the ministry and to those who might have received from the ministry. Jesus Himself did not enter ministry until the voice from Heaven was spoken. The voice of the father in ministry is needed to confirm the son's ministry.

A son must manifest such a life that reflects his father in ministry and brings honor to the office. This is why the phrase "let no man despise thy youth" is followed by this exhortation:

> *...but be thou an example of the believers, in word, in conversation, in charity, in spirit, in faith, in purity. Till I come, give attendance to reading, to exhortation, to doctrine. Neglect not the gift that is in thee, which was given thee by prophecy, with the laying on of the hands of the presbytery. Meditate upon these things; give thyself wholly to them; that thy profiting may appear to all. Take heed unto thyself, and unto the doctrine; continue in them: for in doing this thou shalt both save thyself, and them that hear thee* (**1 Timothy 4:12-16**).

There will always be those who "despise government. Presumptuous are they, self-willed, they are not afraid to speak evil of dignities" (2 Pet. 2:10). "Likewise also these filthy dreamers defile the flesh, despise dominion, and speak evil of dignities" (Jude 8). "Whose mouths must be stopped, who subvert whole houses, teaching things which they ought not..." (Tit. 1:11). The real losers are those who do not receive sons. It shows that they never received the father either. "That all men should honour the Son, even as they honour the Father. He that honoureth not the Son honoureth not the Father which hath sent Him" (Jn. 5:23). We need to honor our fathers. One way is to honor the son sent by the father.

A son honoureth his father, and a servant his master: if then I be a father, where is Mine honour? and if I be a master, where is My fear? saith the Lord of hosts unto you, O priests, that despise My name....

       Malachi 1:6

Chapter 11

The Father's Honor

I quickly crossed the parking lot and entered the yellow brick building through the front glass doors. The sterile white hallway stretched out before me like a hopeless highway. Strange mutterings and confused cries tugged at my heart as I passed door after door. I always feel this strange, sad blending of compassion and resigned reality each time I come to the rest home to be with my dad.

Room 56 always comes up much too soon and I've noticed an involuntary hesitation each time I approach that yellow varnished door. Time has used her tools well and I know that once again my memory of the wonderfully strong and gentle man is about to be repossessed by the truth of this moment.

Today he is in a wheelchair. Stiff at the hips and knees, he sits somewhat slumped on his side, but secured in that positions by a bed sheet tied around his upper body. He was fumbling with the knob when I came into the room. Without any sign of recognition, he asked me to "deliver him from this terrible bondage." Then he looked up at me again and with enormous emotion said, "Well, Luke ... Where have you been? I've been out looking for you all night!" (Luke is his older brother.)

"Daddy, this is Mark." He answered, "Oh, yes," and as he pulled my hand toward his face, he kissed it over and over and softly began to weep. Struggling through the fog of his advancing dementia, he knows me. I am Mark. I am his son.

Slumped in that chair, battling to stay awake in my world, is the man who pioneered and established more than 20 churches. Here is the brave heart who, at my age, sold our farm, furniture, tools, and toys to move to a spiritually barren part of the northeast and begin again because he "couldn't find anyone younger who would go."

Often when I'm with my dad, we sing old hymns and quote Scripture together. If I get it going, he can almost finish it. Alzheimer's has taken his mind, but the Holy Ghost still has his heart!

The Father's Honor

I have cited this very personal experience for several reasons, all of which I want to expand upon in this final chapter. First of all, I am not visiting and caring for my father because of anything he can give to me or do for me. As a matter of fact, for many years now, I have been blessed with the privilege of providing a good portion of my mother and father's support. Furthermore, there is no inheritance to be gained by my attention to my parents. They have no savings, real estate, or treasures to pass on. The reason for my unending devotion, care, and support is simply *honor.*

Secondly, it seems impossible to me that a man or woman of God could be basically destitute in those sunset years after imparting so much into the lives of others. Of course I know the stock religious answer is that a ministerial organization or fellowship should be responsible. But in all my scriptural research, I have never come across any such pattern or illustration.

Before man decided to help God by creating all these synthetic religious remedies, there was and still is a powerful spiritual plan to care for and sustain the elders and fathers of the faith. The real issue is not the lack of a pattern, but rather the lack of courage to change and embrace God's plan rather than man's. Remember, man's religion always dies screaming!

The first time I was interviewed by the state health care staff concerning my father's failing physical condition and the possibilities of assistance with some care facility, the questions went something like this:

"What is the total amount of your father's monthly income?"

I explained that together, my father and mother received something less than $500 each month from Social Security.

The next question was, "Well, what about their savings?"

My answer was that they had none.

"All right, then lets discuss their real estate holdings."

To this I responded, "They own nothing."

"Did you bring their insurance policies?"

Again my answer was negative. "They have no insurance."

Taking off her glasses and looking up at me, the lady impatiently asked, "Well, just what *do* they have?"

Without thinking I responded, *"They have a son...they have me."*

Without premeditation, I believe I had not only voiced a natural principle, but had in fact struck at the heart of a powerful spiritual concept. The inheritance of the sons eventually should become the inheritance of the fathers. Here is the manifestation of *honor*.

There are reasons for why we often lack double-portion anointings and miss true spiritual inheritances. Financial blessings and adequate Kingdom funding is no haphazard coincidence. The Bible is a book of blessings and cursings. In other words, if we obey, we are blessed; if we disobey, we are cursed. So perhaps we should scripturally state the case. God says that the relationship between fathers and sons *must* come into order to prepare for the manifestation of Jesus and the Day of the Lord. "Behold, I will send you Elijah the prophet before the coming of the great and dreadful day of the Lord: and he shall turn the heart of the fathers to the children, and the heart of the children to their fathers, lest I come and smite the earth with a curse" (Mai. 4:5-6). Please note the end of the verse: "lest I come and smite the earth with a curse."

Forgive me if I appear bold and direct, but again there are reasons we have an inordinate number of totally out-of-order ministries. A great many of these are self-ordained or organizationally sponsored, and without a clue to their true parental identity or responsibility. These ministries are not only orphaned and fatherless, but they are often illegitimate, abused, and neglected as well.

Since we are looking at the father-son relationship issue from the perspective of the father's honor, let's focus on the father's position.

I think of Paul, the apostle who penned more than half of our New Testament. Languishing in lonely, filthy prisons, cold and destitute, this father of churches, elders, and other apostles pleaded with his son Timothy to "please bring me the cloak I left at Troas" (see 2 Tim. 4:13). This man, who had clothed so many, needed to be clothed. At the end of his life and by his own admission having "finished my course" (2 Tim. 4:7), he finally stated in grave resignation, "no man stood with me, but all men forsook me" (2 Tim. 4:16).

David is no doubt the most beloved warrior of all the Bible. His youthful victories over bears, lions, and giants intrigue and thrill us. His struggle with Saul is tragically classic. But even more glorious is the tenacity with which he endured those 15 long years from the oil to the gold!

Finally, crowned thrice at Hebron, David established the kingdom, made Jerusalem the "city of David," and raised up a tabernacle of praise to Jehovah.

The years passed, carrying with them the aroma of pleasant and gracious living. From time to time, in David's life as in our own, the aroma became a stench. Life is not just the collection of good times, but rather the amalgamation of all things (good and bad) that "work together for good to them that love God" (Rom. 8:28). David sinned, allowed continued iniquity among his sons, and indulged in a series of bad decisions-and God still said that he was a man after His own heart (Acts 13:22).

Here I want to briefly address the issue of the father's past baggage. Sin must never be covered, but true repentance must never be ignored. Judging by the example of the fathers of the Bible, perfection was rare, and misconduct a familiar cohort. Realignment was always the godly criteria for continuance. Fathers do not become non-fathers because of their less-than-perfect lives or activities. If that were the case, then there would be no more fathers and, consequently, no more sons! As always, however, refusal to repent and turn remains the all-encompassing disqualifier.

Do not forget Noah, the most righteous man God could find in the earth at that time. Remember that his obedience, against all reason, delivered one human family during the time of God's displeasure and wrath. Then remember that Noah sinned. He planted a vineyard and drank from his own success. Ham, his son, seeing his father weak and disadvantaged, threw honor away and got for himself and his seed a curse. Shem and Japheth, on the other hand, honored and covered their father and in turn received blessing. (See Genesis 9.)

Concerning David, Second Samuel 21:15 states, "Moreover the Philistines had yet war again with Israel; and David went down, and his servants with him, and fought against the Philistines...." The familiar ground of battle seems to be a constant in the life of David. The episode we now refer to is not very different from all the others, except that this time we are told that the great warrior, who in times past rejoiced in the battle and exalted in the fray, now "waxed faint." The Scriptures go on to show that Abishai, one of the sons of Israel, smote and killed the particular Philistine tormenting David. "Then the men of David sware unto him, saying, Thou shalt go no more out with us to battle, that thou quench not the light of Israel" (2 Sam. 21:17b).

There comes a time when fathers can no longer labor in the same way or strength that made their sons love and adore them in times past While life and desire may still burn bright in their hearts, their days of active service eventually wind down. They are left to leading the troops from afar. Someday a father will have to stay in a small, closed-in room, longing for a cloak before the winter arrives. This covering should be brought by the one who has been covered by this man's fatherhood and oversight: a son. There is a time when the inheritance of the sons is turned back to the fathers. This is honor.

The word *honor* occurs 146 times in 136 verses of the Bible. This word in the original language seems to denote the power of an attitude toward someone that not only views him as glorious or great, but actually makes him that way by a submitted, respectful response.

Exodus 20:12 states, "Honour thy father and thy mother: that thy days may be long upon the land which the Lord thy God giveth thee." Jesus quoted Moses by saying, "Honour thy father and mother" and then added, "He that curseth father or mother, let him die the death" (Mt. 15:4).

In Matthew 15, Jesus rebuked the religious leaders of His day for their lack of honor toward fathers:

> *But He answered and said unto them, Why do ye also transgress the commandment of God by your tradition? For God commanded, saying, Honour thy father and mother: and, He that curseth father or mother, let him die the death. But ye say, Whosoever shall say to his father or his mother, It is a gift, by whatsoever thou mightest be profited by me; and honour not his father or his mother, he shall be free. Thus have ye made the commandment of God of none effect by your tradition. Ye hypocrites, well did Esaias prophesy of you, saying, This people draweth nigh unto Me with their mouth, and honoureth Me with their lips; but their heart is far from Me. But in vain they do worship Me, teaching for doctrines the commandments of men* **(Matthew 15:3-9).**

These words from our Savior refer to a theological loophole the Pharisees created to subvert the plan of God in the name of God and maintain their greedy lifestyles and a religious appearance at the same time. If a father was in need and asked his son for support, the son could simply say, "Corban," or, "It is a gift." This magic phrase placed any requested property or funds as "set apart for God" and untouchable for secular use by anyone except the present owner, who would "hold it" for God for an indefinite period of time. They would not honor their father or mother, considering themselves to be free and having no responsibility.

This is similar to the attitude of ministry people today who show no honor to anyone as a father in their ministry. Leaning on false understanding, we negate and paralyze the commandments of God in our relationships by excusing a father's need. We either blame him for not playing the game of "preach and pay" successfully enough, or we quote pseudo-faith statements like, "He is God's man; let God take care of him."

Jesus then quotes Isaiah, showing us that giving honor is not a matter of saying nice things, but having a heart toward the person. The manifestation of honor is something offered in the arena of our human ability to give, to show, or to make substantial. A true manifestation of honor is necessary, not simply giving lip service. We must honor our parents not merely in our feelings, but also by our actions. Isaiah prophesied, "...This people draw near Me with their mouth, and with their lips do honour Me, but have removed their heart far from Me, and their fear [or respect] toward Me is taught by the precept of men" (Is. 29:13). Not only do the traditions and precepts of men cancel the fear and the honor that is to be given to God, but they also cancel the fear and honor that is to be given to spiritual and natural fathers.

Those who do not give this honor are usually buried in a sense of pride. Those who carry such pride state or manifest the idea that they actually need no one. More significantly, in their pride they seem to say that what they have is the result of their own doings rather than from anything they received. Proverbs 15:33 teaches that there is a certain attitude necessary for honor to be present: "The fear of the Lord is the instruction of wisdom; and before honour is humility." Proverbs 18:12 says, "Before destruction the heart of man is haughty, and before honour is humility." Proverbs 22:4 says, "By humility and the fear of the Lord are riches, and honour, and life." So we must assume that the lack of honor is also the lack of humility, and that the lack of humility most always indicates the presence of enormous pride.

Remember: "For though ye have ten thousand instructors in Christ, yet have ye not many fathers" (1 Cor. 4:15a). It is so easy for us to gain instruction and understanding from a multitude of sources, yet find no place in our lives to bestow honor. God is requiring in this day, in order to lift the curse that has fallen upon Kingdom people that we locate and acknowledge by more than lip service those who have gone before us. These fathers who set government, order, and foundations into our lives are to be honored. Again, the manifestation of honor, something offered in the arena of our human ability to give, seems evident in Scripture.

Not only does it seem evident, but the Scripture also gives direction as to how honor should be manifested. Proverbs 3:9 says, "Honour the Lord with thy substance, and with the first-fruits of all thine increase." Honor and substance seem to be synonymous.

Since we have spent some time talking about King David in these pages, we might also look at First Chronicles 29:28:

The Father's Honor

"And he died in a good old age, full of days, riches, and honor...." Second Chronicles 1:12 states," Wisdom and knowledge is granted unto thee; and I will give thee riches, and wealth, and honour...."

Concerning Jehoshaphat, Second Chronicles 17:5 says, "Therefore the Lord stablished the kingdom in his hand; and all Judah brought to Jehoshaphat presents; and he had riches and honour in abundance." Notice that riches and honor go hand in hand. One goes with the other.

Thus the word of the Lord, "This people honour Me with their lips, but their heart is far from Me," seems to state that lip service is given, but there is no presentation of riches. When Nebuchadnezzar was going through his enormous dilemma, he called for someone to bring him the interpretation and answer to his dreams. He says, according to Daniel 2:6, "But if ye shew the dream, and the interpretation thereof, ye shall receive of me gifts and rewards and great honour: therefore shew me the dream, and the interpretation thereof." Furthermore, Nebuchadnezzar's recognition of God's ability to speak into his life is met with the statement in Daniel 11:38: "But in his estate shall he honour the God of forces: and a god whom his fathers knew not shall he honour with gold, and silver, and with precious stones, and pleasant things."

The understanding of giving honor as the giving of financial support is stated the most clearly in the instruction of the apostle Paul: "Honour widows that are widows indeed" (1 Tim. 5:3). Again, in reference to ministry, he says, "Let the elders that rule well be counted worthy of double honour, especially they who labour in the word and doctrine. For the scripture saith, 'Thou shalt not muzzle the ox that treadeth out the corn. And, The labourer is worthy of his reward" (1 Tim. 5:17-18). Honor that is only given by lip service is no honor at all. Throughout Scripture there is an overwhelming amount of evidence that honor carries with it the presentation of wealth—including gold, silver, precious stones, pleasant things, etc.

Now you can see more clearly why, in Malachi 1:6, the theme of this chapter is pronounced by God.

A son honoureth his father, and a servant his master: if then I be a father, where is Mine honour? and if I be a master, where is My fear? saith the Lord of hosts unto you, O, priests, that despise My name. And ye say, Wherein have we despised Thy name? **(Malachi 1:6)**

Here the priests show no remorse and reveal that they have no clue as to their responsibility to God. As long as they say they honor God, they assume all is well, but God says that His name is being despised. Further on in Malachi we read, "Bring ye all the tithes into the storehouse that there may be meat in Mine house, and prove Me now herewith, saith the Lord of hosts, if I will not open you the windows of heaven, and pour you out a blessing, that there shall not be room enough to receive it" (Mal. 3:10). In other words, God is saying that He is willing to lift this curse from not receiving honor if we will bring presentations or manifestations in the form of tithes and offerings. This will open the windows of Heaven and begin the flowing out of blessings upon our life.

Second Chronicles 32:27 tells us about King Hezekiah, who "had exceeding much riches and honor: and he made himself treasures for silver, and for gold, and for precious stones, and for spices and for shields and for all manner

The Father's Honor

of pleasant jewels." Now we also understand that Hezekiah made a tragic error by showing these blessings to his enemies-and eventually they were lost when Jerusalem was taken by Nebuchadnezzar. These and other indignities are only exceeded by the attitude of those who assume that honoring themselves is the highest form of honor that can be given.

Nowhere is this stated clearer than in the Book of Esther, in the story of Mordecai and Haman. Mordecai had done a great service for King Ahasuerus by uncovering a plot to take the king's life and by giving the warning that saved the king. The king, wanting to do something special for Mordecai, called in Haman and asked him, "What shall be done unto the man whom the king delighteth to honour?" Haman thought in his heart, "To whom would the king delight to do honour more than to myself?" (See Esther 6:6.) Thinking that the honor belonged to him, Haman answered the king that "royal apparel, one of the king's own horses, and a crown should be delivered to one of the king's most noble princes, that he might array the man whom the king wants to honor. Then the noble should lead him on horseback through the streets of the city and proclaim before him. 'Thus shall it be done to the man whom the king delighteth to honour.' " (See Esther 6:8-9.) Haman is still thinking that he should receive this honor. To his chagrin, the king named Mordecai as the recipient of this honor and then appointed Haman to be the chief prince to lead him through the streets. Esther 6:11 says, "Then took Haman the apparel and the horse, and arrayed Mordecai, and brought him on horseback through the street of the city, and proclaimed before him, Thus shall it be done unto the man whom the king delighteth to honour."

This story shows the spirit of so many in our setting today who can think of no one to honor but themselves. Men who have Kingdom influence assume that all honor belongs to them. It is from this attitude that para-church ministries and church organizations assume the place of fathers in the lives of others. This is stolen honor-all because of an attitude of pride.

These recipients of blessings also assume that whatever they get, from whatever source, belongs to them. Hence we have what Jeremiah said: "Therefore, behold, I am against the prophets, saith the Lord, that steal My words everyone from his neighbor. Behold, I am against the prophets, saith the Lord, that use their tongues, and say, He saith" (Jer. 23:30-31). Without even so much as "Thanks," they steal themes, thieve messages, and proclaim revelations that they "borrow" from lesser-known men, proclaiming that they themselves received those things from God by revelation. No father begrudges his son anything that is in his house. No man of God is offended by someone in relationship borrowing inspiration, repeating revelation, or using spiritual ideas that were handed down through proper relational channels. A son does not have to feel that he is a thief to use his father's things. A thief is someone who slips in by night under the cloak of treachery and pronounces that the things he has in his house are his own, when he took them from others. That man is not only a thief, but a liar.

So much of the supposed revelation and inspiration being spread around today are words and themes hewn out by prayerful men and women who gave their lives for those things. They went through an enormous process in order for

The Father's Honor

those things to come into being, only to see them taken away by Hamans in the Kingdom who assume that the honor really belongs to them.

A true son has a right to all his father's goods by inheritance. As long as he honors his father and gives a manifest reason for using those things, they are never withheld from him. But outside of father-son relationships, any fruit taken from another man's tree is stolen honor. Such "borrowers" have not followed the scriptural precept to give "honor to whom honor is due" (see Rom. 13:7). With weighty revelations and truths hanging on their branches as fruits that did not come through the root system of their own process, they will eventually become too heavy and the tree will fall over.

King Saul's undoing was that he had no problem in taking Samuel's place. He just assumed that because he had kingdom influence, he had the right to offer sacrifice. God's response to that was, "to obey is better than sacrifice, and to hearken than the fat of rams" (1 Sam. 15:22).

Second Chronicles 26:18 records the story of Uzziah the king, who was smitten by leprosy because he assumed he could burn incense unto the Lord in the office of a priest:

> ***"And they withstood Uzziah the king and said unto him, It appertained not unto thee, Uzziah, to burn incense unto the Lord, but to the priests the sons of Aaron, that are consecrated to burn incense: go out of the sanctuary, for thou hast trespassed; neither shall it be for thine honor from the Lord God."***

Uzziah took honor that belonged to the sons of Aaron.

Gehazi saw no reason why he should not receive

garments and silver from Naaman even if Elisha, for some strange reason, turned down such generosity. What is the harm in receiving gifts from a healed Syrian?

> *But he went in, and stood before his master. And Elisha said unto him, Whence comest thou, Gehazi? And he said, Thy servant went no whither. And he said unto him, Went not mine heart with thee, when the man turned again from his chariot to meet thee? Is it a time to receive money, and to receive garments, and oliveyards, and vineyards, and sheep, and oxen, and menservants, and maidservants? The leprosy therefore of Naaman shall cleave unto thee, and unto thy seed forever. And he went out from his presence a leper as white as snow* (2 Kings 5:25-27).

The father heart of Elisha was turned toward Gehazi, but Gehazi's heart was turned toward attaining wealth. Gehazi's crime was not simple disobedience against a prophet's desire, but the receiving of riches that Elisha refused. In this, Gehazi stole the honor due his spiritual father. Again we see here the equation of money and honor. Again we see the judgment of God against those who steal honor. Because the skin is the covering of the body, when dishonor is committed against spiritual covering, judgment is received in the area of the offense.

God's plan for the care of fathers is laid out in type in the priesthood. The Lord spoke unto Moses:

> *Thus speak unto the Levites, and say unto them, When ye take of the children of Israel the tithes which I have given you from them for your inheritance, then ye shall offer up an heave offering of it for the Lord, even a tenth part of*

the tithe. And this your heave offering shall be reckoned unto you, as though it were the corn of the threshingfloor, and as the fullness of the winepress. Thus ye also shall offer an heave offering unto the Lord of all your tithes, which ye receive of the children of Israel; and ye shall give thereof the Lord's heave offering to Aaron the priest Out of all your gifts ye shall offer every heave offering of the Lord, of all the best thereof, even the hallowed part thereof out of it. Therefore thou shalt say unto them, When ye have heaved the best thereof from it, then it shall be counted unto the Levites as the increase of the threshingfloor, and as the increase of the winepress. And ye shall eat it in every place, ye and your households: for it is your reward for your service in the tabernacle of the congregation. And ye shall bear no sin by reason of it, when ye have heaved from it the best of it: neither shall ye pollute the holy things of the children of Israel, lest ye die **(Numbers 18:26-32).**

Note that God is offering to give credit to those who give tithes as though they have given everything. He does so because they are willing to obey God in giving the tenth part. This goes back to a principle that I call "the like-as principle." God is God and He can call "those things which be not as though they were" (Rom. 4:17). He is able to say, "Since you owe Me everything and I require from you everything, not just a tithe, I am going to make a deal with you. If you will give Me what I ask, a tithe, a tenth, then I will reckon it in My accounting as if you gave Me everything: all the corn and all the wine." What a glorious, blessed God we serve.

In Numbers 18:28 He goes on to say, "Thus ye also

shall offer an heave offering unto the Lord of all your tithes which ye receive of the children of Israel: and ye shall give thereof the Lord's heave offering to Aaron the priest." Aaron was the high priest. He was the father of the sons of the priests.

Reread verses 29 through 31:

Out of all your gifts ye shall offer every heave offering of the Lord, of all the best thereof, even the hallowed part thereof out of it. Therefore thou shalt say unto them, When ye have heaved the best thereof from it, then it shall be counted unto the Levites as the increase of the threshingfloor, and as the increase of the winepress. And ye shall eat it in every place, ye and your households: for it is your reward for your service in the tabernacle of the congregation (Num. 18:29-31).

In other words, God does not really count the tithe the people give to the pastors or to the Levites until those pastors heave up to the high priest, or to the apostle, or to their fathers, a tenth part of their own tithe. A tenth part of the tithe received of the people belongs to Aaron the high priest.

The high priest in the Old Testament is equivalent to the apostle in the New Testament The author of Hebrews uses both New Testament and Old Testament terms in the same sentence when he says that Jesus is "the Apostle and High Priest of our profession" (Heb. 3:1). They both serve as an overseeing father in ministry. So then this "tithe of the tithe" was to be heaved up to the high priest (in our New Testament understanding, to the apostle or father of a ministry), in order that the tithe of the people be blessed.

Is it possible that much of the problem we are having

with our church finances can be traced back to not offering a tithe of the tithe to the father of a ministry? Is it possible that the blessings we promise to the people every week as we receive their tithe, such as "You will be blessed and will prosper," because they are honoring God with their tithes and offerings, are based on following an order that we have ignored? Is it possible that this blessing is cut short because we have not honored God with our own tithe?

Most pastors tithe back into their own churches; hence they are paying themselves. That is not tithing up. The New Testament story in the Book of Hebrews concerning Abraham and Melchisedec says that Abraham paid tithe of all to Melchisidec, and hence the lesser paid tithe to the greater (see Heb. 7:2,7). Tithing must always go up so the connection can be made all the way to the head. When the oil is poured out on Aaron, it is poured on his head so it can flow all the way down to the skirts of the garment (see Ps. 133). Leaving fathers out leaves a disconnection; then when the oil is poured out on headship, it does not flow all the way to the skirts of the garment.

Jesus made this statement: "He that receiveth you receiveth Me, and he that receiveth Me receiveth Him that sent Me" (Mt. 10:40). This seems to be a theme in His ministry, as He stated further in John 5:23: "That all men should honour the Son, even as they honour the Father. He that honoureth not the Son honoureth not the Father which hath sent Him." So you can see here that a connection is made between fathers and sons.

In John 8:48, Jesus was accused of having a devil. He answered, "...I have not a devil; but I honour My Father, and ye do dishonour Me" (Jn. 8:49). Then, in John 8:54, He explains, "...If I honour Myself, My honour is nothing: it is My Father that honoureth Me; of whom ye say, that He is your God." Here Jesus says that His honor really is not His own, but comes to Him from His Father, or flows down from above.

To further show that honor flows down through the relationship between fathers and sons, Jesus states in John 12:26, "If any man serve Me, let him follow Me; and where I am, there shall also My servants be: if any man serve Me, him will My Father honour." In other words, if you serve Jesus, you not only get the blessing of Jesus, but also the blessing of the Father that flows down through the Son.

Pause here with me to reflect a moment. How many men and women of God have given their lives to the gospel, raised up churches, raised up sons like my own dear father did, and now die in dishonor and poverty? How many men and women are still desperately trying to hold on and serve in pulpits and ministry places when they themselves know their efforts are less than adequate? They continue simply because they would have no means of income or support if they stopped.

The Scripture teaches that the high priest should not serve in the tabernacle past 50 years of age.

> *And from the age of fifty years they shall cease waiting upon the service thereof, and shall serve no more: but shall minister with their brethren in the tabernacle of the congregation, to keep the charge, and shall do no service. Thus shalt thou do unto the Levites touching their charge* **(Numbers 8:25-26).**

He does not carry pans or basins. He does not light

candles or pour incense anymore. Rather he goes out and sits in the gate as a counselor and an elder in the city. This would be impossible for the ministry in our day. Their only source of livelihood is derived from their ability to continue to minister. Hence we have weakened the ministry and closed the gates of blessing.

I realize that what I am stating here will be criticized. I understand that many will be offended, especially those who are proud. But borrowed waters and stolen inspiration are rampant in our Church world today. Men understand that when they get older and less useful, there is nothing left for them. Therefore, instead of seeking biblical remedies, many are willing to beg, borrow, or steal to gain enough wealth before they are too old to effectively minister. Houses, cars, clothes, and goods need to be gained while they are young and strong-at any cost—because there is no inheritance for them when they are older. We must make the inheritance that was given from the fathers to the sons into an inheritance given back, at some point, as honor to the fathers.

I am reminded of the story of Saul. Before he became king of Israel, he was just a young man sent out by his father to search for lost asses. When he could not find them, he decided, along with his servant, that there must be somebody who had some wisdom in God who could give him direction. "And he said unto him, Behold now, there is in this city a man of God, and he is an honorable man; all that he saith cometh surely to pass: now let us go thither; peradventure he can shew us our way that we should go" (1 Sam. 9:6). Saul, who at this time was humble and without arrogance, told his servant that he really could not go to this man and ask him anything because they had no "present to bring to the man of God" (1 Sam. 9:7). He would not take the man's revelation without offering something back. The servant, according to verse 8, answered Saul again and said, "...Behold, I have here at hand the fourth part of a shekel of silver: that will I give to the man of God, to tell us our way." I think we should remember that Saul, before he was proud and arrogant enough to take the place of the priest, would not even request spiritual direction without offering something material, a manifestation of honor, to the man of God.

The Book of James declares, "Behold, the hire of the labourers who have reaped down your fields, which is of you kept back by fraud, crieth: and the cries of them which have reaped are entered into the ears of the Lord of Sabaoth" (Jas. 5:4). Our spiritual fathers have pioneered the frontiers of Kingdom experience for us. They handed down to us areas of revelation for which we paid nothing, but cost them everything. The Lord of hosts hears the cries of old men and women who languish in apartments, hospital rooms, and in trailer homes. He hears those who have given their lives for the gospel, those who we in turn have handed over to the government and the state. We cannot proclaim "Corban" and pretend that a debt of honor does not exist. We should reclaim these golden vessels in their golden years. Perhaps we should go back and remember that if they are our fathers, we owe them honor.

After the wicked reign of Athaliah, Joash came out of his seven years of hiding to rule in the land and bring a great revival and reform to the house of God. The house of the Lord had been neglected, and there were huge gaps in its structure. Joash began a rebuilding project to restore the Lord's temple to its proper order:

The Father's Honor

And Jehoash said to the priests, All the money of the dedicated things that is brought into the house of the Lord, even the money of every one that passeth the account, the money that every man is set at, and all the money that cometh into any man's heart to bring into the house of the Lord, let the priests take it to them, every man of his acquaintance: and let them repair the breaches of the house, wheresoever any breach shall be found **(2 Kings 12:4-5)**.

The priests failed to perform the words of the king.

But it was so, that in the three and twentieth year of king Jehoash the priests had not repaired the breaches of the house. Then king Jehoash called for Jehoiada the priest, and the other priests, and said unto them, Why repair ye not the breaches of the house? now therefore receive no more money of your acquaintance, but deliver it for the breaches of the house. And the priests consented to receive no more money of the people, neither to repair the breaches of the house **(2 Kings 12:6-8)**.

There is a terrible breach in the household of God. Fathers in the ministry have not been given proper honor. They poured out their lives, but are receiving nothing back. We should never wait until a spiritual father is unable to provide for himself before we give him honor. This gaping hole in the relationship between fathers and sons is the wound of fathers who constantly flow a stream of life to sons, and sons not flowing honor back to them. Fathers are to provide the generational link for the impartation of mantles in double portions. A son is to pour water on the hands of his ministry father before he is ever separated from him. The imperative of ministry today is to bridge the generation gap between father and son in the ministry.

The Lord promised to send a curse on the earth. A curse will come unless there is a turning, not only of the fathers toward the children, but also of the children toward the fathers. "And he shall turn the heart of the fathers to the children, and the heart of the children to their fathers, lest I come and smite the earth with a curse" (Mal. 4:6). Unless we repair the breach in the wall, there will be a constant breach in the Spirit. The Lord may also say to sons who have not honored their fathers, "...now therefore receive no more money of your acquaintance, but deliver it for the breaches of the house."

There is always a breach when the Lord's voice is ignored and His will unobserved. This breach of the Lord is made against a good man named Uzzah. He died because he tried to do a good thing, but he was in the wrong order.

> *And they set the ark of God upon a new cart, and brought it out of the house of Abinadab that was in Gibeah: and Uzzah and Ahio, the sons of Abinadab, drave the new cart. ... And when they came to Nachon's threshingfloor, Uzzah put forth his hand to the ark of God, and took hold of it; for the oxen shook it. And the anger of the Lord was kindled against Uzzah; and God smote him there for his error; and there he died by the ark of God. And David was displeased, because the Lord had made a breach upon Uzzah: and he called the name of the place Perezuzzah to this day* **(2 Sam. 6:3, 6-8).**

He died trying to steady an Ark that was carried in an oxcart pattern of the world, instead of on the shoulders of the priest. The resting place of Deity is supposed to be in this order: "...and the government shall be upon His

The Father's Honor

shoulder.... Of the increase of His government and peace there shall be no end....upon His kingdom, to order it, and to establish it with judgment and with justice from henceforth even for ever..." (Is. 9:6-7).

The only place of proper government, order, and pattern is upon the shoulders of the priesthood. To carry the burden of the Lord in any other way is death. Good intentions can never replace God's order. Sons have allowed their fathers in ministry to carry the complete weight of their office upon their own shoulders. Fathers were never meant to do that alone. It is an improper order.

"For because ye did it not at the first, the Lord our God made a breach upon us, for that we sought Him not after the due order" (1 Chron. 15:13). David discovered the order of the priesthood and realized that Uzzah died, not because God is cruel, but because He demands that the revealed order of His will be obeyed.

Good men are suffering today in a breached order that does not give honor where honor is due. Unless the sons of a ministry father follow the "due order" of God, we will continue to have a ministry that is "out of order," disconnected from inheritance and unable to birth true ministry.

We are in danger of God's bringing a "breach of promise" curse against us: "After the number of the days in which ye searched the land, even forty days, each day for a year, shall ye bear your iniquities, even forty years, and ye shall know My breach of promise" (Num. 14:34).

If we do not honor our fathers, we will stay in the wilderness until a generation arises that will obey the voice of the Lord.

> *...To day if ye will hear His voice, harden not your hearts, as in the provocation, in the day of temptation in the wilderness: when your fathers tempted Me, proved Me, and saw My works forty years. Wherefore I was grieved with that generation, and said, They do always err in their heart; and they have not known My ways* **(Hebrews 3:7-10).**

If the heart of the fathers turns to the children, and the heart of the children to their fathers, the earth and the Church will be free of the curse. If we have a father in the ministry, where is his honor? Is it being held in escrow, until full inheritance is received? Or are we refusing to honor where honor is due? "Render therefore to all their dues: tribute to whom tribute is due; custom to whom custom; fear to whom fear; honour to whom honour" (Rom. 13:7).

We must follow the order of God in carrying the burden of ministry. Fathers cannot carry the blessing of God alone. If sons will honor their fathers in ministry, we can restore the breach in the house of God.

> *And they that shall be of thee shall build the old waste places: thou shalt raise up the foundations of many generations; and thou shalt be called, The repairer of the breach, The restorer of paths to dwell in* **(Isaiah 58:12).**

> *In that day will I raise up the tabernacle of David that is fallen, and close up the breaches thereof; and I will raise up his ruins, and I will build it as in the days of old* **(Amos 9:11).**

Until that day.

CPSIA information can be obtained
at www.ICGtesting.com
Printed in the USA
BVHW092239240822
645456BV00006B/17